HOW TO BULLET-PROOF YOUR MANUSCRIPT

HOW TO BULLET-PROOF YOUR MANUSCRIPT

BRUCE B. HENDERSON

Cincinnati, Ohio

Publisher's Note:

This book covers only the broad general principles set forth herein and is not intended to be an exhaustive legal treatise on these subjects. The author is not an attorney and does not purport to offer legal advice. Specific problems invariably involve individual considerations and should be promptly referred to legal counsel.

How to Bulletproof Your Manuscript. Copyright © 1986 by Bruce B. Henderson. Printed and bound in the United States of America. All rights reserved. No part of this book may be reproduced in any form or by any electronic or mechanical means including information storage and retrieval systems without permission in writing from the publisher, except by a reviewer, who may quote brief passages in a review. Published by Writer's Digest Books, 9933 Alliance Road, Cincinnati, Ohio 45242. First edition.

Library of Congress Cataloging-in-Publication Data

Henderson, Bruce B., 1946-
   How to bulletproof your manuscript.

   Includes index.
   1. Libel and slander—United States. 2. Authors—
Legal status, laws, etc.—United States. I. Title.
KF1266.H4   1986   345.73'0256   86-24538
ISBN 0-89879-233-9   347.305256

Design by Joan Ann Jacobus

CONTENTS

PREFACE

Writers need to learn how to limit their legal exposure and protect their pocketbooks and reputation. Forewarned writers are prepared writers.

1

TARGETING A TOPIC

Evaluate your topic to judge how tempting a legal target it's likely to make you.

2

DANGER AHEAD: WHAT YOU'RE UP AGAINST

Grounds for suit: libel, defamation, invasion of privacy, plagiarism. The red-flag areas where only verifiable facts can protect you. Pornography/obscenity and "contemporary community standards."

3

CONTRACT-SIGNING BLUES

The dreaded "Indemnities and Warranties" clause; if you're sued, what will the publisher do for you, and *to* you? Interpreting what specific contract provisions really mean. Negotiating for a better deal.

4

RESEARCH MAKES (AND SAVES) A WRITER

Effective research through libraries and public
and government records. Prove your facts and guard
against unintentional copyright infringement (plagiarism).
Fair use and seeking permission to quote.   **29**

5

THE HUMAN FACTOR: SOURCES AND INTERVIEWS

Finding and interviewing sources. Guarding against
prejudiced or unreliable sources. Finding backup
sources for extra verification. Interview strategies.
Handling confidential sources—how far should you go to
keep them confidential? Kinds of sources: named, not for
attribution, background. Don't let yourself be manipulated
by your sources.   **39**

6

PROTECTION FOR THE FICTION WRITER

Handling fact-based characters and events to avoid
lawsuits. The special problems of "faction." Legal and
marketing considerations of obscenity/pornography.   **51**

7

WRITING AND EDITING TIPS

Resisting the impulse to invent "facts" or doctor quotes. Paraphrasing accurately. Not quoting out of context. Not letting the new fictional techniques distort the truth in nonfiction. Unauthorized biographies. Assembling your notes, writing the piece. Final bulletproofing before submission. Handling editorial suggestions.   **59**

8

COPYRIGHT, PERMISSIONS, AND RELEASES

What's copyright? How long does it last? How can you get permission to quote copyrighted material? When there's infringement on *your* copyrighted material, what should you do? Using affidavits. Prepublication agreements with subjects you profile. Collaboration agreements. Agreements with researchers. Model releases for photos. The dangers of generic photos. Getting permission to reprint photos.   **65**

9

FACT-CHECKERS AND LAWYERS

Working with a publisher's fact-checkers and legal department to protect against legal troubles later. Keeping your background documentation—how much verification is enough? Confirming quotes. Trivial mistakes can imply carelessness about the important facts too.   **77**

10

THE LAWSUIT

You've done everything right . . . but you're still sued.
What the publisher does. What you do. How you can get
free or low-cost legal counsel. Ground rules to follow
during a suit. You're responsible for what you wrote,
even if you were quoting. Claiming privilege—qualified
or absolute. Fair comment and criticism. Proving
malice. What if you were wrong? Retractions and
corrections. Who can sue for invasion of privacy? What if
the publisher sues you to get back the advance?   **85**

11

INVESTIGATIVE REPORTING

Smelling a rat and hunting it down. Targeted
investigations are very likely to become targets for
lawsuits, but they're one of the most exciting fields in
journalism. Fundamental research for investigative
reporting to find out facts indirectly, without alerting
your subject. Sorting through accusations. Using off the
record and insider sources, including "whistle blowers."
Records and documentation. The Freedom of Information
Act. How to know if what you smell is really a rat or just a
red herring. Confronting your target. Undercover
investigative methods.   **91**

12

Final Dos and Don'ts

Avoiding libel (written), a writer can blunder into slander (spoken). The protection words: *allegedly* and *reportedly*. The red-flag words you should watch out for. Alertness, accuracy, and common sense are the basic bulletproofing tools that will help keep you out of legal trouble. **101**

PREFACE

Every byline is a possible lawsuit. I say this not to dissuade anyone from writing professionally. Quite the opposite is true, as I have helped train hundreds of writing students in the courses I've taught at three California universities in the past eight years. I simply wish to make life safer and more profitable for those talented and dedicated enough to pursue writing as a craft and as a business. I attempt to do this by showing writers how to limit their legal exposure and protect their pocketbooks and reputations. My goal: Forewarned writers should be prepared writers.

Unfortunately, in the last decade or so, writers have increasingly become targets of suits alleging libel, defamation, and invasion of privacy, as top magazines and book publishers encourage us to get under the surface with our writing and to find controversy in our subjects. Part of the blame for the rising numbers of legal suits (in all areas of the law) must be charged to the ever-growing pool of hungry lawyers in this country. Take this one alarming statistic: there are more lawyers in the County of Los Angeles than in the entire country of Japan. Indeed, filing lawsuits has become a way of life in the United States. People sue their business partners, relatives, neighbors, employers, creditors, doctors, and even their lawyers. How can we, as writers, expect to be treated any differently?

Some lawsuits filed are justified; many are not. Either way, having to defend against a lawsuit—even a frivolous one—can be expensive and exhausting for a writer. To date, the legal defense tab for my writing career is approximately $60,000—all but a couple of thousand dollars paid not by me, for which I am thankful, but by the publishers involved. I've been sued three times; all three actions were dismissed prior to trial, yet in the amount of time I spent in legal defense, I could have written a string of articles or another book.

Ironically, the most expensive lawsuit against me—costing some $40,000 in legal fees—was brought against me by a convict, who, using the extensive law library at Terminal Island Federal Penitentiary in southern California, prepared his own legal arguments and acted as his own attorney. I had written an article for *Esquire* about this individual's $10 million bank embezzlement caper, a story which also resulted in a book contract for me to expand the tale. Among other things, the prisoner sued for interruption of business; his business, he claimed, was being a federal inmate. *Esquire's* well-heeled New York City law firm hired a top-flight Los Angeles firm to make court appearances in California, and soon, the bicoastal legal bill soared into the stratosphere. When the suit was eventually dismissed by a U.S. District Court judge, the *Esquire* publisher wrote a column about it, hailing the outcome as some important journalistic victory. Meanwhile, my book publisher got a terminal case of cold feet at the idea of paying to defend the book against a similar suit threatened by this stubborn (and smart) criminal, and shelved the project just a few weeks after I had delivered an 80,000-word manuscript. Some victory for me, huh? Actually, it was my feeling that the win belonged to the guy behind bars, as he managed to keep from print a book about his crime. (And just where were my rights to sue him for interrupting *my* business?)

The best idea, of course, is not to get sued in the first place. And I know as a fact that the practical methods I have developed over the years to bulletproof my work have prevented other lawsuits from being filed against me. My personal troubleshooting formula for avoiding litigation offers no foolproof guarantee, of course, as evidenced by the lawsuits that have been filed against me. In fact, an appropriate subtitle for this book might be "Notes From a Bullet-Riddled Writer." In this country, *anyone* can sue *anybody* for just about *anything.* But my efforts have not only reduced the number of times I've had to go to court, but they have also kept me from ever *losing* once I ended up there. Both are worthy goals for a writer at work in today's litigation-happy society.

I did not dream up this bulletproofing formula. I came across it the hard way—by spending long, tedious times with editors, researchers, and lawyers, discovering where I'd made mistakes and learning how to correct them.

To all of those experts who helped save my skin through the years, I owe my thanks—as do you. For in these pages, you'll be hearing from them indirectly, as I share with you my legal experiences, both good and bad. By learning "how to bulletproof your manuscript," you'll be reducing your chances for legal exposure and increasing the likelihood that your writing will be both enjoyable and profitable.

Good luck. (It never hurts.)

B. B. H.
March 1986

1

TARGETING A TOPIC

Entire volumes have been written about finding salable ideas for fiction and nonfiction stories and books. There's room for more, and I encourage you to read them all; armed with the knowledge of what sells, you're on the road to being a successful professional writer.

Here, however, I'll be outlining ways to analyze your topic early on from another critical standpoint: *How tempting a legal target will it make and what can you do to start protecting yourself?* It is not premature to ask yourself this tough question You must not allow yourself to write with blinders on. Unlike the skittish race horse who is afraid of the cheering crowd, you need to know exactly who is out there and who might be ready and willing to pounce on you.

Don't get me wrong—just because a topic is possible fodder for a lawsuit doesn't mean you should abandon the idea. Indeed, some of today's best articles and books have been potential targets for lawsuits, and their authors have known it from the beginning. In fact, with today's interest in controversial subjects, the fact that your topic is potentially litigious might make it more, not less, salable. As an example, take this call I received a couple of years ago from the editor of *California* magazine:

"We want a piece on the worst judges in the state," he said. "Interested?"

"Who decides which ones are the worst?" I asked.

"You do. Let's name them and blow the lid off." (Young magazine editors talk like this. Unbeknownst to this one, I had proposed a bad-judges article to his predecessor a few years earlier. At times such as these, though, it's best to let the editor-in-control think the idea is his baby.)

It was a big story with big headaches. In print, "Court Jesters" named and pictured seven judges we called "California's worst judicial embarrassments." About one judge, I wrote: "Dictatorial and intimidating." About another: "Frequently drunk on the bench; biased." We named an additional five judges to our "Dishonorable Mention" list and selected three former judges to our "Hall of Shame."

Two of our "worst judges" held press conferences the week the article came out and publicly threatened to sue. "I look forward to owning that magazine someday," promised one offended jurist. A major complaint the other judge had was that I had reported his height at 5' 3", while he alleged to be 5' 7". (Okay, I didn't pull out a tape measure, but I'm 5' 6" and I looked down at that man.)

In the end, no judge sued. (In fact, "Shorty" resigned from the Superior Court bench two weeks later.) The reason we were not sued was that we had been careful to check and recheck all our facts. (Repeat after me ten times: *Truth* is the best defense against libel. *Truth* is the best defense. . . .) The important process known as *fact-checking* will be dealt with in another chapter, but let me make this point now: *The magazine and I both knew this topic was a potential legal nightmare, and we took steps from the beginning to protect ourselves.* Writers should do this with *every* topic they write about nowadays.

Most assignments do not originate from editors over the phone, of course. Even established writers are expected to generate the bulk of their own ideas and approach an editor by sending a well-constructed query letter to a publication. And don't think book authors do it any differently. In the book business, a publication contract and advance royalties result from a proposal (essentially, a long query), which generally consists of an outline and sample chapters. Queries and proposals should be informative and entertaining. Also, they should be accurate and objective. If you are later sued, both you and the publisher may be ordered to turn over your complete working files to the plaintiff. That would certainly include your query, as well as everything that followed. If you've written, "I've never liked this SOB—let's get him," then you should seriously consider moving to Katmandu. Such an admission would undoubtedly show bad intentions on your part and help the plaintiff recover monetary damages. Many, if not most, libel suits hinge on the legal issue of *malice*—that is, did the writer recklessly disregard the truth? Or did the writer deliberately set out to defame someone? If the answer to either of these questions is yes, then even the tiniest mistake in a published work can lead to the writer's losing a libel suit. For these reasons, you must be careful about in-progress memos sent back and forth between you and your editor. No intelligent, conscientious editor would write, "How's your piece on that SOB going? Hope you've dug up some dirt on him." Don't you get caught writing anything similar, either.

That doesn't mean that you can't be explicit and detailed when you have the goods on someone. In fact, to get higher-paying assignments, you need to do just that. Take this excerpt from a query I wrote to my editor at *Reader's Digest,* which resulted in an assignment and a published article ("Mighty Mite vs. the Porn Queen," March 1986):

> *I have an idea for an article dealing with the efforts of the federal government—and one woman U.S. prosecutor in particular—to put out of business and behind bars California resident Catherine Wilson, who at the time of her arrest last year, was believed responsible for distributing a whopping 80 percent of the child porn in the United States.*
>
> *Cathy Wilson lives in a classy Los Angeles neighborhood called Hancock Park and drives a Rolls Royce. Such luminaries as Muhammed Ali and Mayor Tom Bradley live nearby. Though officially unemployed and on welfare, Wilson single-handedly ran her distribution outlet, selling Scandinavian-produced titles like "Lollypops," "Children-Love," and "Lolita-Sex" through the mail to a list of five thousand customers with a special taste. Using the pseudonym "Jackie Steen" and a Denmark post-office box, Wilson would hit the road monthly in her Rolls, mailing her packages of smut from towns*

throughout Arizona and New Mexico, never using the same mail drop more than once a year. She was able to make in excess of $500,000 a year—all of which she hid in bank accounts in the Cayman Islands. The phony name, the European postal box, the offshore bank accounts—all of it accomplished what Wilson set out to do: confound U.S. investigators.

To get that kind of information for a query, you obviously have to do some work. One of the first things you'll want to determine is whether or not the topic has ever been done before. Your first stop should be your local library. The *Reader's Guide To Periodical Literature*, which you will find in the reference collection, is a good place to start. This book catalogues article subjects published in hundreds of magazines since 1900. For my bad-judges story, I found a magazine story that had rated judges in Los Angeles. To look up book topics, go through *Books In Print* at the library or any bookstore; you'll find books listed by subject, author, and title. Here, I found a fine book, Joseph C. Goulden's *The Benchwarmers,* which identified the worst federal judges in the country.

Also, you should look for old newspaper articles written on the same or a similar topic. Many libraries keep back issues of the local newspaper on microfilm. If your library doesn't, then go to the newspaper office and see if they will let you look through their index and clipping morgue. This is where I found a slew of articles about the kiddie porn peddler, and from them I got much of the information I needed to write the query. (For financial reasons—remember, time *is* money—I use as much information as I can from existing articles in order to write a query. Once I get the assignment, I use that same information as a jumping-off point to start my own serious research.)

As you start to zero in on a topic, make sure to keep an eye open on the legal front. For instance, I considered it a plus to find that other writers had judged some of the judges I had chosen to write about. If, later, I wrote about a judge who had already been labeled a baddie by another writer, then I would at least have company. However, using previously published material in no way protects you from being sued for libel. (Indeed, when *Reader's Digest* reprints an article from a leading publication that has already checked the facts in its story, the *Digest* staff nonetheless double-checks everything as if they were starting from scratch.) Publication lawyers, though, do like it when you tell them that other writers have rapped someone you're rapping, particularly when the other writers were never sued or successfully defended a lawsuit.

It's vital to know whether any lawsuits resulted from the earlier articles or books. If you suspect its legal history (especially when you have chosen a particularly controversial topic), contact the publication. Speak to a staffer in the newspaper's or magazine's editorial or research department, and try to talk to the reporter or writer as well. What can they tell you? I'll tell you what I told two writers who called me when they came across my piece in *Esquire*. One writer was from a German publication, and the other was on assignment for a computer magazine; both were doing articles on the litigious bank embezzler. (You see, just because a topic has been done before doesn't mean that you should avoid it. Oftentimes, topics that have been done before are among the most salable.) I said something like, "This guy has taken a vow to sue anyone who writes about him. So, double-check all your facts, and make sure your publisher is ready to pay the legal bills." (By the way, a writer will usually cooperate with another writer if it doesn't take up too much time—time is money to a freelance—and as long as their stories or interests are not competitive.)

You can also check for any lawsuits in the civil court records in the city where the subject and author live. Unfortunately, this type of checking cannot usually be done by mail but must be accomplished in person. So, in order to pull this off, you have to have a guarantee from the publication for expense money so you can travel to the city or hire a local person to search the court files. (If your subject lives in a faraway city, you might have to wait and do this after you have the assignment, unless you have a friend, relative, or colleague living in the area who will not charge you for a trip to the courthouse.) If a suit has been filed, the subject's name will be found in the plaintiff's index, while the writer or publication will be listed in the defendant's index. The court file will usually indicate the possible problem areas with the story and will show whether any judgment was rendered—in other words, did the writer or plaintiff win?

If a topic has encountered previous legal difficulty, find out the exact nature of the problem. If the writer simply made a stupid mistake and was vulnerable to a legal challenge, you still might want to go ahead, making sure you don't commit similar mistakes. Or, for that matter, make any new mistakes. Covering some topics, however, practically guarantees a lawsuit. If you label as a crook a successful businessman who has a clean criminal record, you will probably be sued. Even if your charges are true, the businessman might feel that he has nothing to lose. Maybe with a sharp lawyer and some mistakes on your part—or your attorney's—he can win some sort of vindication in court. Such a story should be written only if you can uncover some solid proof to back up your statements, and you have someone footing the expense of your legal defense, because even if what you write is true, you will have to prove it in court if you are sued.

Always check your own motivations for doing a story. If they involve revenge or anger, skip the topic. Revenge would go directly to the malice issue, and anger would cause you to lose your objectivity and make some major mistakes. That's not to say that you can't care about your topic: it might seem difficult to be objective about a convicted child pornographer, for example. But allowing the facts to stand on their own and writing in an evenhanded manner—while being informative and entertaining, of course—is what professional journalism is all about.

If this suggested regimen sounds like too much work to do before getting a commitment from a publisher, just remember that the more complete your query, the better the chances that you'll interest an editor. I consider a magazine query worth two or three days of work. This would include not only the early work at the library, but also telephone interviews (they are easier and quicker than face-to-face ones) with important subjects or sources—people you can quote in your query. A nonfiction book proposal takes me a minimum of two to three weeks because the package needs to be much longer, more detailed and finely tuned. Novelists (even published ones) writing fiction find it difficult to get contracts without writing the entire book, an inequity I've never fully understood or accepted.

During this preliminary work, I have to make an important decision: I have to analyze everything I've learned and decide whether or not I want to go ahead with my idea. If I put a couple of days into a magazine topic and still see huge holes and seemingly unsolvable problems in it, I'll usually cut my losses and forget it. Even when you get the assignment (usually you won't because the editor will see the same holes and problems that you do) and complete the article, you'll probably still find those difficulties haunting you. This has happened to me a couple of times—and they represent the only kill fees I've received in sixteen years of magazine writing.

After I put my time into a query and I'm convinced that the topic will sell, that I'll enjoy doing it (happiness not to be underrated in life), and that I can back myself up legally, I send my idea to ten magazine editors simultaneously, hoping to get at least one offer. If I get none, then I send it off to ten more editors before even considering giving up. If I get more than one offer, then I usually write for the highest bidder. (All of the same holds true for book proposals; I expect my agent to show it to at least ten book editors, hoping to get more than one bidder.) Sending out simultaneous submissions is standard operating procedure for writers who know what they're doing. After all, in sending a query or proposal to a publisher, you're not agreeing to write the article or book. Such a mutual agreement would only result after a discussion of money and the signing of a contract. By circulating your proposal, you're simply trying to determine which publishers are interested in holding such discussions with you. Until you've signed a contract, you're free to discuss and consider writing for anyone. (Interestingly, I've found that it helps rather than hurts my reputation with a publisher when I say, "Sorry, someone else is paying me more.")

If an editor is interested in the topic but concerned from a legal standpoint, you will probably get a phone call. "How can we prove this?" the editor might ask. (They often use the editorial *we* when they actually mean *you*.) The nature of your response may be crucial to your chances of securing the assignment. Don't fake it, just show them what a firm handle you already have on the story and how aware you are of the legal ramifications, thanks to those days you put into researching the topic and analyzing it as possible grounds for a lawsuit. Tell the editor what you can prove now and what you think you can prove after you do some work on the topic. But don't let the editor talk you into doing that work for free. You've given them their free look at the story in the form of a query. If they want to know the end of the story, they should have to pay for it.

Okay, let's say you did everything right and you get the assignment or the book contract. Congratulations.

Now your legal problems begin for real.

2

DANGER AHEAD: WHAT YOU'RE UP AGAINST

A writer and a publisher lose a lawsuit and are ordered to pay $75,000 for making a fictional character too similar to an actual person.

Two writers and their publisher lose a multi-million-dollar lawsuit for writing and circulating a memo that contained damaging information about someone.

A publishing house sues a writer for $138,000, claiming it had been misled by the writer into publishing libelous material.

An author loses a court judgment for falsifying a real sports figure's personal background in writing a "fictionalized" account of his life.

These are not hypothetical scenarios. They are actual cases from the nation's court dockets. It is scary stuff because it hits close to home for all writers, whether they write fiction or nonfiction.

There are lessons in these and other cases. First, writers must realize the power they have within their craft. When I first started in the business, my father liked to remind me: "The pen is mightier than the sword." And indeed it is. We have at our fingertips the ability to do great good when we succeed and to cause great harm when we fail. So, why shouldn't we be held strictly accountable for our professional actions?

I have no intention of writing a legal text. However, writers need to be aware of the specific legal areas that affect them every time they set words to paper. In the succeeding pages, I'll be covering these areas in detail and offering some practical methods for avoiding those legal pitfalls that occasionally claim a writer. By way of a quick overview, here's some of what we should be trying to guard against in our writing:

Libel. This is the most common type of suit filed against writers. Simply put, libel is doing injury to someone's reputation. More exactly, it is doing damage to someone by publishing false information with malicious intent.

Defamation. This is a separate tort that is libel's close cousin. It is the act of destroying or impairing someone's good name or character or livelihood.

Invasion of privacy. The principle of law involved here holds that *private people* have a right to lead a private life without being exploited by publishers and writers. When they are so exploited, it becomes an *invasion of privacy.* In Chapter 10, pp. 88-89, there are guidelines on how to tell public people from private ones.

Plagiarism. Using substantial portions of another writer's work without authorization in your own text and representing it as your original work.

We will also discuss *copyright,* which is the ownership of one's writing. It protects you from having others steal your work—known both as plagiarism and as copyright infringement—and stops you from doing the same to other writers.

Freedom of the press is, of course, a most sacred right in this country. It was so important to our founding fathers that they made it the First Amendment to our Constitution. But in recent times, our highest courts have ruled that First Amendment protections are not a "license to circulate damaging falsehoods or personal attacks on a person in the guise of news gathering and informing the public." In other words, there is a limit to the freedom we freely enjoy.

Lawyers for publishers and plaintiffs alike know what those limits are, and so should you. *Any time* you venture into the following areas, you are more vulnerable to a possible lawsuit than if you avoid them. They are:

- *Implying the commission of a crime. Even if a man has been arrested at the scene of a bank robbery with the loot in his hand, he is an accused robber until he is convicted.*
- *Injuring someone in his or her profession or job. If you write that a doctor botched a surgery or a lawyer misrepresented a client, you are potentially costing these professionals business and money.*
- *Stating that someone has a "loathsome disease" that would cause social ostracism. Though this one might sound silly, writers have lost lawsuits for this. Gonorrhea and leprosy are examples from past cases. Nowadays, AIDS would also certainly qualify as a disease that would lead to ostracism.*
- *Damaging someone's credit or financial standing. Writing that someone was slow to pay a bill or ducked out on a debt altogether would certainly qualify.*
- *Implying a lack of chastity. Most publication lawyers would undoubtedly agree that mention of almost any sexual activity—short of criminal assaults and molestations—does not belong in a nonfiction story or book, even if it is true, unless the subject openly admits to such activity.*
- *Indicating a lack of mental capacity. Someone you call dumb might be just smart enough to hire a lawyer and sue you for everything you're worth.*
- *Inciting public ridicule, hatred, or contempt of an individual.*
- *Claiming that a subject associates with organized crime. Writing that someone belongs to the Mafia is a good way to end up in court, as numerous investigative reporters have found out.*

So, you've noted the above and said to yourself, "Boy, I'm never going to do any of that stuff." Well, in my writing career, I've ventured into most of the above red-flag areas. The lesson here is not that you should avoid these areas, but that in order to protect yourself, you should have *verifiable facts* whenever you cross into the danger zone.

And what does "verifiable" mean? "Preferably two or three sources," says one publishing attorney. "Documented records and evidence is always better than hearsay and interviews. A writer should keep in mind that if other people go through his file to see what he based his factual conclusions on, are they going to think that he was reasonable in concluding what he did? If not, the writer might be in trouble."

Before a writer loses a lawsuit, the law usually requires that it be proved in court that the writer willfully wrote untruthful things or showed reckless disregard for the truth. In legal terminology, this is called *malice*. While the question of what constitutes malice continues to be argued in the highest courts, the following evidence has, in the past, established actual malice on the part of publishers and writers of nonfiction (and cost them dearly in legal fees and damages):

- *The writer fabricates an interview or source. This is an obvious call, but it has certainly been done before and will unfortunately be done again.*
- *A statement of fact is actually the product of the writer's imagination.*
- *Information in an article is based wholly on an unverified, anonymous telephone call.*
- *The article contains an allegation that is so inherently improbable that only a reckless person would put it into circulation.*
- *Something is published despite obvious reasons to doubt the veracity of the source of the information.*

Unlike the laws involving libel, which are reasonably clear, the laws encompassing *pornography* and *obscenity* are confusing at best but must be mentioned. Almost annually, it seems, the U.S. Supreme Court comes out with a new ruling that changes the existing legal interpretations. We know this for sure: obscenity is *not* protected by the Constitution. It never has been and, I say unequivocally, never will be.

What is less clear is trying to define obscenity. A landmark decision that was handed down some thirty years ago left it up to the "average person applying contemporary community standards" to determine whether or not a book or a film was obscene. So, even to this day, what is obscene in Peoria may not be obscene in New York City. Cities and towns throughout the land are using local zoning ordinances to confine or eliminate "obscene" material from their local bookstores and movie houses. And in most cases, the Supreme Court upholds their right to do so.

Writers have a difficult time second-guessing what will be considered obscene *somewhere* by *someone*. One author at a local writers' conference lamented to his colleagues the banning of his book in a southern state for "obscene" language. The offending word: a four-letter description for flatulence. So, you can see, we're not just talking about *Lady Chatterley's Lover* here. If your writing is ever banned for being obscene, there are plenty of legal support groups that you can go to for (free) help. And a few more guidelines for exploring this murky and confused realm are offered in Chapter 6.

If you're about ready to hock your typewriter or computer and take up a new calling, wait a minute. You don't have to be a lawyer or enjoy living and breathing legalities in order to properly protect yourself. And it should be the business of every writer writing today to know exactly how to do so.

3

CONTRACT-SIGNING BLUES

Some of you might be laboring under the misconception that getting a contract in the mail is fun. Wrong. Repeat after me: Getting a *check* in the mail is fun. Unfortunately, though, you can't have the kicks of the latter without enduring the former.

Contracts are never pleasant to wade through—if you find them so alluring, then I suggest you think about going to law school. But even those of us with little interest in the law and less interest in lawyers must learn how to wade through contracts. Why? Because virtually everything in a contract affects us in one way or another; usually either financially or legally.

There are people you can go to for assistance. Agents and lawyers are the obvious choices, but experienced writers who have been through the process before can also give helpful tips and recommendations.

In most instances, professional writers *don't* use agents to make sales to magazines but *do* use them to peddle book proposals. This is so because there isn't enough money in magazine fees these days to justify giving a percentage to an agent. With a new *Writer's Market,* we can stay on top of the magazine industry—know who's buying what and for how much—better than an agent who is concentrating on book and film deals.

The book business, though, is still largely based in New York—where most literary agents are located or should visit regularly—and is by nature an insular industry. Deals and contacts are made over lunch and drinks. Agents pick up industry gossip: this publisher is looking for nonfiction crime and that publisher is hot for romance novels.

Unfortunately, there are some crooks in the literary-agency business. Understand that when you sell a project through an agent, it is the agent and *not* the writer who receives the money (all of it) from the publisher. An ethical agent will do what my agent does: he deposits the publisher's check in his agency's account, then quickly issues a check for the sum received from the publisher less his 10 percent agency commission. (The industry norm is a 10 percent commission, though some agencies charge as much as 15 percent.) You can imagine what an unethical agent might do. Holding onto your money for a month or two to solve a cash flow problem at the agency is just for starters, and the possibilities get worse from there. Since the last thing you want to do is sue an agency in order to recover your money, keep these things in mind when selecting an agent to represent you:

- *Good agents have shelves of books by clients. Get the names and phone numbers of a few, and call them as references. If there are no shelves of books or clients, beware.*
- *Editors will recommend agents they have successfully worked with in the past. In fact, I found my current agent on the recommendation of two book editors during a trip I made to New York.*
- *Keep informed about everything your agent does. Know how much money you have coming and when. Agents have lots of writers and lots of things happening at any one time, so don't let them lose you in the shuffle.*
- *Another thing the publisher will send to the agent and not to the writer is the royalty statement. Be sure your agent sends you a copy of the statement. Also, review it carefully, and make sure all the numbers add up.*

Back to the contract. Two copies of it are sent to you—or your agent if you have one. Unless your agent is also a lawyer, you should not look in his or her direction for legal advice. An agent's expertise and experience rest in the financial arena, such as what rights should be retained by the author and what percentages of the income you should receive for the rights you do sell.

Every book publisher around requires a writer to sign a contract. And more and more magazines are following their lead these days. Few contracts are simple and direct; most are long and complicated. Since they are written by lawyers, how could we expect anything different? When you're going over a contract, the following are some things to keep in mind:

- *Take the contract at face value.* Unless you and the editor agree to a deletion and both initial same, you are bound by every word and clause and legal meaning in the contract. Don't believe an editor who advises you to sign an objectionable contract because it's "just for the attorneys." I did once, though I had balked at a clause that explicitly stated that the magazine would not necessarily defend me in case of a lawsuit. "We defend all our writers," the editor said proudly. When we were sued, the publication's lawyers decided it was a conflict of interest to defend me, and I had to hire my own lawyer for a short period of time before the case was dropped.

- *Verbal agreements should become riders to the contract.* Your only real protection is being guaranteed something in writing. For instance, I have gotten a few publishers to sign an agreement stating that they will defend me in case of a lawsuit. Now that I've said that, let me admit that such a guarantee is difficult to get. However, verbal agreements can be legally binding. The problem is proving who said what to whom. If you have made an important verbal agreement, you should memorialize it by writing a letter or statement that sets out the points of your agreement. The names of the person or persons involved in the agreement should be indicated, and your statement should be signed, dated, and sent to the person with whom you have the agreement. You should include a line that says something like, "If this does not accurately reflect our agreement, please notify me at once." The implication should be clear: if they don't notify you, then this is your agreement.

- *Take the contract to your own lawyer.* Depending on the topic of your article or book and the degree to which you think it might be a target for a lawsuit, it may be wise to show your contract to an attorney who specializes in publication law. In a situation like this, you should not go to a divorce lawyer or personal-injury specialist, as you might be bringing them the first book contract they've ever seen. Publication law is involved and ever-changing, so you'll want to talk to a lawyer who understands it and makes a living out of staying on top of the latest developments.

Once you find the right attorney, make sure you spell out exactly how much you can afford to spend. Make sure the lawyer agrees to stay within your announced budget. Otherwise, you might get a bill that exceeds your article fee or first advance payment.

What you want from a lawyer is a learned opinion on certain key clauses, most of which I usually find impossible to read even though they appear to have been written in my native language. Try this on for size, which comes word-for-word from a Doubleday book contract I signed:

> 22. (a) Author shall indemnify and hold Publisher harmless from any claim, suit, or action, and any expense or damage in consequence thereof, asserted by reason of Publisher's exercise or enjoyment of any of its rights hereunder or by reasons of any warranty or indemnity made by Publisher in connection with the exercise of any such rights, as provided in subparagraphs (b), (c), (d), and (e) hereof.

Don't think those subparagraphs make any more sense. But all this mumbo jumbo has to mean something, you say. I took the contract to a publication lawyer, who read it and announced that every word of the contract was written to protect the publisher, not me. In short, if we ever got sued, I was in big trouble.

In plain English, here's what all those subparagraphs meant if anyone filed even the most frivolous, groundless lawsuit against us:

- *The publisher could choose his own counsel.*
- *I would have to pay half the publisher's legal costs.*
- *The publisher could withhold all of my royalties. If the suit was more serious—as it would be if I had committed factual errors, for instance—and we ended up with legal liabilities, then, in addition to the above, the following could happen:*

- *If the publisher settles the suit out of court, I must pay half of any amount the publisher agrees to pay the plaintiff.*
- *If we lose the lawsuit, I have to reimburse the amount of money the court or jury ordered the publisher to pay in damages, plus pay any damages I was ordered to pay.*

I sat down and reviewed my options. If any two of these five clauses were invoked, I would have no choice but to:

- *Commit hari-kari.*

So, why did I sign the contract? Because I wanted to be published. With the "Indemnities and Warranties" clause, the publishers are usually unwilling to compromise. Almost anything else in a publishing contract is highly negotiable, but this killer section is written in granite by the publisher's team of skilled lawyers out to protect the publisher, not you. If you do not agree to it, they will not publish you. Period and end of discussion.

About the time we were trying to negotiate on some of these points with Doubleday (I had my lawyer talking by phone to Doubleday's lawyers), a Doubleday editor whispered a horror story to me. When Edmund Muskie, the former presidential candidate and U.S. Senator from Maine, was negotiating with Doubleday for his memoirs, he reportedly also balked at the "Indemnities and Warranties" clause. Muskie flew to New York in the company of his attorneys—not one but a handful. They spent a week in New York, the editor continued. And the net result: *not one word* of the clause was changed. Needless to say, my lawyer did no better than Muskie's guys.

Inevitably, magazine contracts will contain a version of the "Indemnities and Warranties" clause. This from *Reader's Digest*:

> *You warrant that you own the rights conveyed herein or are the copyright owner's duly authorized Agent, that you have the full power to grant such rights, that the Work does not infringe any copyright or rights of any third party, or contain any matter that is libelous or otherwise in contravention of law.*

More simply put, but just as important. While there's nothing there about having to pay the legal bills and so forth, the magazine is asking you to promise that you didn't plagiarize (steal from) someone else's work, and that you didn't libel someone. If you did either, or broke the law in any other way in connection with writing the article, the magazine has the right to sue you for breach of contract and probably a host of other claims. Of course, that does not exempt the publisher from a suit for libel or plagiarism—it just threatens to make life more difficult for a writer who gets the publisher into such a legal jam.

An editor at another magazine once put it even more simply: "If you screw up, we'll come and get you." And there have been cases of magazines and book publishers doing just that—suing writers whose serious errors of judgment in the researching and writing of an article or book resulted in lawsuits.

However, if you don't ask, you won't get anything. So, it doesn't hurt to request changes in the "Indemnities and Warranties" clause. For example, I asked Doubleday for coverage under their legal insurance policy—covering both legal bills and monetary damages—something that a number of book publishers had already done by that time. "We're not covering our writers yet, but we'll soon be doing so," my editor reported. As a result of my request, the following clause was added to my contract: "In the event that Doubleday adopts a policy of insuring its authors against libel prior to the publication date of this work, that policy shall apply to the undersigned Author retroactively." And sure enough, a few months later and before my book was published, I received notification that I was duly covered by Doubleday's insurance policy, as Doubleday became the latest publishing house to join the tide in helping to protect writers. The rider that was added to my contract included the following points:

- *The Author shall be an additional named insured only with respect to the Work or Works that are the subject of this agreement.*

- *The Policy limits of liability are $5 million for each occurrence and $5 million annual aggregate.*

- *The Policy deductible is $50,000 for each occurrence. Coverage is for loss under the Policy for amounts in excess of the deductible but not greater than the Policy limits.*

- *The Author shall be responsible for the deductible as follows:*
  1. *In the event of loss due to any claim, suit, or action for obscenity, libel, or violation of any right of privacy, then (10 percent) of the total advance under this agreement, but not less than five thousand dollars ($5,000) or more than twenty-five thousand dollars ($25,000);*
  2. *In the event of loss due to any claim, suit, or action for plagiarism, piracy, errors or omissions, infringement of any proprietary right at common law or any statutory copyright, or any other claim, suit, or action not covered in subclause above, twenty percent (20 percent) of the total advance under this agreement, but not less than ten thousand dollars ($10,000) or more than fifty thousand dollars $50,000).*
- *The Author agrees to completely and fully cooperate with the Publisher and its counsel in the defense of any claim, suit, or action brought against the Publisher and/or Author concerning the exercise of rights under this agreement. Should the Author fail to cooperate, it shall be construed as a breach of this Agreement, which could result in the loss of the insurance protection provided hereunder.*

This insurance rider is amazingly clear and speaks for itself. The amounts of the deductible and the limits of the policy vary slightly from one publisher to another, but the above figures are fairly standard.

The same thing is true with asking magazines for changes in their "Indemnities and Warranties" clause. Listen to this writer's experience: "The magazine sent me the contract and the editor said to cross out anything that I found offensive. I did. I crossed out the indemnity clause, only warranting that the article was original. As I said to my editor, 'How can I state that anything does not infringe upon another's rights, particularly in this day of sue-happy attorneys and willing litigants?' I sent the contract back, but my version was unacceptable, and back came another contract. What I finally got them to cross out was important: that I would not indemnify the magazine against any loss, damage, or expense. In other words, if they are sued because of my article, I'm not responsible financially. I also inserted the words 'to the best of my knowledge' in the sentence stating that the article was not libelous." In this case, the writer was successful in changing the "Indemnities and Warranties" clause to be more favorable. While I wish I could report that this was a trend in publishing, I'm afraid it is not.

The American Society of Journalists and Authors, an organization of 800 leading freelancers, recommends several ways that an "Indemnities and Warranties" clause can be changed to reduce the potential risks for a writer:

• Insist that the indemnification clause apply only to breaches ultimately sustained by a court judgment, and not also to *alleged* breaches. (Filing a lawsuit and winning one are two different things. Why should a writer be declared in violation of the indemnification clause just because some joker sued? A lawsuit could result in all your royalties being withheld until it is eventually decided.)

• Indemnify the publisher only against "reasonable and actual attorneys' fees"; you don't have to get stuck paying $500-an-hour legal fees, which most judges and courts would find "unreasonable."

• Seek to limit your liability to the amount you are paid for the article or book. (Why, even in the worst scenario, should you lose more money than you made on the project?)

• Obtain the right to defend any action brought against the publisher to which your indemnification applies with counsel *of your own choosing.* (Mainly, this is so that you won't get stuck paying the sky-high legal bills of the publisher's lawyers. But also, as long as you're going to be contributing to the legal bill, it's nice to have your own attorney, who will be responsive to your calls and letters.)

I will add a few of my own suggestions:

• Try to get an "examination of records" clause. It should stipulate that anyone you designate can examine the publisher's records, not just an account, and that if an error is found in excess of 5 percent in terms of money owed to the author, the publisher must pay for a complete audit.

• The "option clause" is not to the advantage of the author. Here's the option clause from my Doubleday contract: "Author hereby agrees that Publisher shall have the first option to publish Author's next full-length book, but in no case shall Publisher be required to exercise this option within three months following publication of the work which is the subject of this Agreement." You can see how this could have tied up my book writing career for some time to come, inasmuch as Doubleday did not release my book until nine months after I turned in the final draft of the manuscript. My agent negotiated to have the option clause crossed out of the contract, which it was.

- If your book is not published within a set time (one or two years) of the publication date in the contract (or even of the date that you turn in the final manuscript), all rights should revert to the author.

Contracts can and should protect writers, too, particularly in regard to promised payments. In fact, if a publication doesn't have a contract, I send the editor a Letter of Agreement, which covers the most important points of a contract from my standpoint. The following is the Letter of Agreement suggested by the American Society of Journalists and Authors:

Date

Editor's Name and Title
Publication
Address

Dear (Editor's name):

This will confirm our agreement that I will research and write an article of approximately (number) words on the subject of (brief description), in accord with our discussion on (date).

The deadline for delivery of this article to you is (date).

It is understood that my fee for this article shall be $ (amount), payable on acceptance, for which sum (publication) shall be entitled to first North American publication rights in the article. If this assignment does not work out after I have submitted a completed manuscript, a kill fee of $ (amount) shall be paid to me.

It is further understood that you shall reimburse me for routine expenses incurred in the researching and writing of the article, including long-distance telephone calls, and that extraordinary expenses, should any such be anticipated, will be discussed with you before they are incurred.

It is also agreed that you will submit proofs of the article for my examination, sufficiently in advance of publication to permit correction of errors.

This letter is intended to cover the main points of our agreement. Should any disagreement arise on these or other matters, we agree to rely upon the guidelines set forth in the Code of Ethics and Fair Practices of the American Society of Journalists and Authors.

Please confirm our mutual understanding by signing the copy of this agreement and return it to me.

Sincerely,

(signed)

Writer's name and address

Publication
by _____
(name and title of editor)

Date _____

You can tell the difference when the writer is constructing the contract. First and foremost, we are interested in when and how much we are going to be paid. Secondly, we don't even bring up the issue of "Indemnities and Warranties." And lastly, we are concerned about the quality of any editing done to our work, and reviewing same before publication.

Even if you can get one or two favorable clauses in your contract, there will still be plenty of ways things can go wrong for you *if* you are sued. The best plan is to sign the publishing contract with its frightening "Indemnities and Warranties" clause, then take measures in your research and writing that will make it likely that a potential plaintiff will be dissuaded by a responsible lawyer from suing because there is so little chance of winning.

In other words, the only way you can win is by bulletproofing your writing so well that few will even be tempted to take a pot shot. Fear not, it can be done.

RESEARCH MAKES (AND SAVES) A WRITER

Writers have won or lost lawsuits because of the quality of their research. Research properly, and a lawsuit probably won't even be filed in the first place. Research poorly, and you may lose everything—a lawsuit, your professional reputation, and the equity in your home, for starters. Make this your credo: *My best legal protection is accurate researching.*

Obviously, writers don't just research for legal reasons. Every writer of prose needs to do research: none of us is born with an innate knowledge of all possible topics. No amount of fine writing will save the nonfiction writer who gets his facts wrong or the novelist who bases his fiction on misinformation. Knowing where to find accurate information is crucial. There is nothing worse than not being able to write because you need to know something, yet having no idea where to go to get the information.

Editors will often look up from manuscripts and ask: "What kind of back-up do you have for this?" What they want to know is what kind of support the writer has for making a statement or suggesting a scenario. For them, and for their lawyers, the best source materials are *written documents*. Any information in writing that you can produce is considered more verifiable than what you hear secondhand or feel in your bones.

However, just because something has been published before doesn't make it accurate or legally safe for you to repeat. In the eyes of the law, republication of a libelous statement is no different from the initiation of a libelous statement. For instance, just because a newspaper called the mayor a crook doesn't mean you can repeat it in a magazine story, unless you have independent proof that the charge is valid. You can never point your finger at the newspaper and say, "I was just repeating what they said." If the paper committed libel, so did you. (This is also tricky when it comes to reporting or writing about a libel suit. If you spell out the alleged libel when writing about the lawsuit, you could be guilty of republishing libelous material. Most news organizations get around this by being vague: "John Doe is suing *Today* magazine for statements that were published in an article concerning his political campaign.")

Still, published books, magazines and journals, newspapers, internal reports, and unpublished documents such as letters, notes, and diaries can all be useful and valuable in your research. The first thing they do is help inform you about your topic. Next, they give you some names of possible sources whom you will want to contact. And finally, you may wish to quote some material—of course, anything you use in your own writing should be double-checked for accuracy.

Once, on the trail of a con man who had bilked numerous men in an elaborate lonely hearts scam, I was pressing an elderly victim to recall the specifics of some love letters sent to him supposedly by a young woman but actually penned by the bad guy. Try as he might, the old fellow couldn't give me much in the way of details.

"And you say you threw all the letters away?" I asked.

"Yep," he said. "After I figured out what was going on, I dumped the lot of 'em."

I knew that quoting from those letters in the article would be important. It would bring the entire shameless scam to life for the readers. But I also knew that I could not quote a letter unless I had an actual copy of one.

"Where did you dump them?"

"Out back under a tree."

"Out *back?* Show me, please."

"It's rained since then," he said. "They'd be all wet."

"That's okay." Wet letters were better than no letters.

Sure enough, they were still there, in one big soggy pile. I didn't even try to read them, but took my clothes out of my suitcase, threw the letters inside and headed for the airport with my clothes in paper bags. Once home, I littered the living room floor with the mildewed letters and fetched the hair dryer. Two days later, the letters were dry enough to read. Interspersing them throughout my *California* magazine piece, "The Love Bandits: A True Story of Marital Crime" (June 1982), made the tale more colorful and believable. And having the letters in our possession meant that I didn't have to field questions from the magazine's lawyers like: "Are you *sure* the love letters aren't a figment of an old man's imagination?" Here's my proof:

> *My Darling Carl: I got 28 letters and I tore them all up except yours . . . You must remember you are my older future husband (If you want me) and I am a young one under twenty . . . with hot love and deep passion . . . I got a job working as a dancer for four hours a day, in the evenings, and someone stole my dance shoes and clothes . . . so now I am really in a terrible mess, can't work . . . Carl my love . . . could you help me with a loan . . . My true love to you, Linda.*

I like to think of my researching as the kind of effort a tenacious prospector would undertake in search of a gold mine. *Somewhere* out there is something that will enrich my writing—all I have to do is find it. It's a challenge I heartily accept, and I must admit to being part detective and part bloodhound.

Finding people is my forte, especially when they don't want to be found. Here are some of my favorite places to find someone: the phone book (don't laugh), the state department of motor vehicles, property records, voter's registration, the post office, marriage and divorce records. Though it helps to be born curious (okay, nosy), learning investigative techniques is also useful. For instance, county voter-registration records are a particularly good place to locate missing persons. Even people who are trying to avoid bill collectors, process servers, or journalists often wish to exercise their democratic right at election time. And it's amazing how many people put in a change of address with the post office before skipping town—probably because there's always *someone* they like to receive mail from. The forwarding address is yours for the asking by simply sending one dollar and a letter requesting the information, along with the subject's name and old address, to the Postmaster in the city (same ZIP code) in which your subject formerly lived. The post office will keep the dollar and send you the new address.

What does all this have to do with bulletproofing your writing? Legally, an article or book that has holes in it is dangerous. If there's a key source who you think could shed some light on a series of events, but you can't find him, then you should press on diligently with an effective search. Even should you end up not finding the source, if a lawsuit results and the attorney for the other side asks you on the witness stand why you didn't try to find this valuable source who would have cleared his client, you can honestly testify that you did try. For this reason, it's crucial that you write down every step you took during your researching, even when you found nothing. "Voter's registration checked, 1968 to present—nothing." Documenting negative results will also keep you from repeating steps you've already taken and using time that could be better spent doing something you haven't done.

A good starting place for your research is the library, where I earlier suggested you go to see if your topic has been done before. Now is the time to go back there and start building a serious clip file, which most pros do as they begin to research a new project. Those newspaper clips, magazine articles, and books that have been written by others can provide some useful points of reference, but of course, you cannot copy another writer's work.

Let me say that *plagiarism* gets my vote as one of the nastiest words in the dictionary. It's defined as the *taking of another's writing and representing it as your own.* To my classes at the University of Southern California's School of Journalism, I would get their attention by saying, "In my class, plagiarism is punishable by death." And I nearly meant it. Certainly, I would think that the discovery of premeditated plagiarism would be the demise of a writer's reputation, and thereby, career. In the case of my students, it was university policy that anyone caught plagiarizing would be immediately expelled. All writers, beginners as well as veterans, should consider plagiarism as terminal as the bubonic plague.

Unconscious plagiarism is the commission of the same

crime, only unknowingly. It's a writer's nightmare to think that something you read long ago is still bouncing around in your head and suddenly pops out—word for word—when you need it most. Unlikely maybe, but quite possible. And you could still be held legally, morally, and financially liable.

A novelist friend of mine spent a year working on a book, and just before sending the manuscript to his publisher, he asked his wife to read it for the first time. She liked it but said that the story and characters reminded her of *The Ugly American*. My friend, who had no memory of ever reading the book or seeing the movie of the same name, went to the library and discovered that his writing was disturbingly similar to the old classic novel about an American diplomat abroad. Not taking any chances (maybe he *had* read the book years before) my conscientious friend reworked his entire novel.

Alex Haley had a different kind of unconscious plagiarism problem with his bestseller, *Roots*. As reported by attorney Carol E. Rinzler in *Writers Connection*, Haley defended himself in a plagiarism lawsuit by explaining that while working on his epic, "people would surround him after he gave public talks and would press snatches of information into his hand, and that some of these apparently had been copied verbatim from already-published books, and may have found their way into his manuscript. It's hard to believe, considering the volume of work he had that was never accused of being plagiarism, that Haley intentionally stole anything, yet he apparently paid royalties to at least one of these claimants against *Roots*."

Remember, the same laws that protect your writing from being used in an unauthorized manner also protect the work of others. But writers do have the protected privilege of using another's work—with proper credit given—in a "reasonable manner" without having to secure the permission of the author. This is called *fair use*, and *fair* is the key word here. Courts have held that such use promotes intellectual progress and the public's access to information and ideas. But determining what's fair has puzzled writers, editors, lawyers, and judges for years. Indeed, there is a thin line between fair use and copyright infringement. Often, the purpose for which the use was put to is of utmost importance. For instance, fulfilling the public's need to know about an important issue may override the rights of the work's original owner. (This was the theory embraced by the U.S. Supreme Court when it ruled that the *New York Times* could print the Pentagon Papers, which had been stolen from the Defense Department. The public's need to know overrode all other concerns.) Conveying the facts and information and advancing the arts and sciences, as well as the dissemination of historical information, would all be considered fair use in most cases. However, when someone's work is used (or usurped) for strictly commercial purposes, the courts have been strict in considering it *unfair* use, which legally is known as *copyright infringement.* The rule of thumb is that if the use cost the copyright owner money, then the user could be in trouble.

Some publishers have set an arbitrary limit on the length of the excerpt to be used—250 to 500 words. But that can be misleading. For example, would 250 words of a 300-word poem be fair use? By all standards, what I quoted above from *Writers Connection* would be called fair use. In my "fair use," I credited both the publication and the author (which means I did not plagiarize), and I conveyed the facts while not costing the publisher or the author any money in so doing. But if you're ever in doubt about what is fair use, it's best to secure consent from the copyright holder. A sample permission request is included in Chapter 8, pp. 66-67.

In some cases, you might be told by the original publisher that your proposed use of the material is fair and that no permission is granted. Other times, you might be given permission for free. There are times, however, when a permission fee is charged. Permissions people weigh several factors, including how much material is to be used and how important it is to the person requesting it. For example, there might be no charge for using a few lines from a poem in a body of text, but a fee might be charged if just one line of the same poem were to be used as a chapter heading. *Publishers Weekly* reports that fees charged by publishers are negotiable, but that they range generally from $15 to $100 per page of prose and from $5 to $25 per line of poetry, depending on the publishing house and on the factors noted above. (Publishers generally split the fee with the author of the work quoted.) According to *Publishers Weekly,* permissions people generally agree that fewer requests are being granted for free these days and that prices have risen in recent years.

Courthouses are not just places where writers go when they are sued. Many times, I've found what I needed—sometimes desperately—for an article or book at the courthouse; not because I do legal writing, but because the very best documents to use for nonfiction writing are court records. A fair share of fiction writers as well find themselves pulling court records in search of material for their story lines. With certain qualifications, you can quote anything, accurately paraphrased or word for word, from public court records with no fear that it will be used against you in a lawsuit, and your right to do so is protected by a privilege granted by constitutional law. Those qualifications are:

- *Whether it is a civil or a criminal suit, make sure that you quote directly from the complaint and that your account is accurate.*
- *If there has been no final judgment, make it clear that you are quoting from a complaint, that these are allegations and not facts, and that no final disposition has been reached.*
- *Give the target of the complaint a fair treatment, quoting denials and so forth.*

Almost regardless of your subject—whether it's a well-loved obstetrician or a sleazy politician—it's important to check the local courthouse and run the subject's name through the index of civil and criminal cases. (By the way, when a bureaucrat, say a court clerk, refuses to help you obtain information that you are legally entitled to receive, the best way to handle the situation is to ask for his name and the name of his supervisor. A threatened loss of autonomy can be a frightening ordeal for a bureaucrat.) Checking court files is not only a way to get good background material on your subject, but it also tells you whether your subject has ever sued any writers, and that information can be helpful. Say you come across a case in which a politician has sued a newspaper reporter for calling him a crook and *lost*. This guy will probably have a heck of a time suing you for saying the same thing. Combing through court cases is also a good way of finding out if your subject has any enemies. Maybe the obstetrician, after years of wonderful work, has suddenly started appearing in a slew of malpractice cases. Has the good doctor gone blind or senile? Such snooping could justifiably change your entire story from a run-of-the-mill profile to an important exposé.

This happened to me once when I was profiling the board chairman of a fast-growing bank. After working on the story for almost two weeks (with the banker's cooperation), I thought I knew nearly everything about him. He was aggressive and bright and seemed well on his way to the top of the financial world. One day when I was lecturing my journalism class, telling them how vital it is to check the court files, I realized that I hadn't run the banker's name through the courthouse index. An hour later, I did just that and found a number of civil cases against the rising-star banker, accusing him of defaulting on loans and debts and charging him with manipulation of bank stock. There were even judgments against him, meaning that he had lost. So, the story changed overnight from a favorable profile to an exposé about a leading banker who couldn't keep his own financial house in order. Though the banker later made noises about suing me, he never did. Because the story was well-documented by information in court files, legal action on his part would have been futile.

Other public records, such as county property tax rolls, are excellent sources of information, too. (Reporters and writers, of course, have no special right to search nonpublic files. Anything that is open to the public is open to us, and vice versa.) You can find out who owns a particular parcel of land or how much property an individual or company owns. The assessed valuation of the land is also available. As a rule, photocopy any records that you think you'll use in your writing. When editors and lawyers are reviewing your file prior to publication, they would much rather see a copy of the original record than a scribbled notation in your notepad. Even the best journalist can misread something.

Notes certainly have their place in your researching, as not every record can be photocopied. Keep in mind when writing your notes that they may be read by other people: certainly the editor and researcher at the magazine, perhaps publication lawyers, and maybe even judge and jury someday. (But you do not have to make an effort to change your handwriting or print your notes. After all, they are *your* notes.) When researching at the library, for example, it is a good idea to paraphrase copyrighted materials in your notes, rather than quoting from them directly. Later, when you are referring to your notes as you write, the paraphrased copy might help you avoid unintentional plagiarism. There are a couple other important points to keep in mind about note taking:

• *Be thorough.* Note full bibliographical information on books consulted so your information can be double-checked later. Don't make your notes so cryptic that you will later doubt what they mean. Avoid writing them so briefly that you won't remember what it all means two weeks later. If you use symbols and abbreviations, write down a key to their meanings on the lead page. This will aid you in reading your own handwriting, possibly years later.

• *Type your notes.* Typing handwritten notes after you've spent a day researching at the library or courthouse or interviewing a source is a good idea for clarity's sake. This process also allows you to fill out certain details while they are still fresh in your mind.

• *Organize.* Writers should develop their own organizational methods. (My wife can tell what project I'm working on by the nature of the material I have spread out on the couch in my office.) File folders work for dividing material by subject or person. I always make sure to label the front flap of a notebook with subject headings for the information that's contained inside. (I recommend Reporter's Notebooks, which fit easily into pockets and purses. They can be ordered through any major stationery store.) Keep old notes in well-labeled boxes so they can be found months or years later. (You should keep everything for at least three years in order to be sure that the statute of limitations has run out on any possible civil lawsuits. The length of time of these statutes varies from state to state, but after they have run their course, a writer may not be sued over an article or book.)

One final good source of information: the federal government. The Government Printing Office (GPO) has 24,000 titles available on a wide range of topics at minimal cost. You can look up the titles in the *Monthly Catalog of U.S. Government Publications* at your library. There are two dozen GPO outlets in the United States (just look in your telephone book under "United States Government"), but when the locals don't have a title you want, write to Government Printing Office, Washington D.C.

There is an old belief in the legal profession. A bookish lawyer who excels at researching is said to be an ideal *back-room attorney*—meaning that he can get along fine without ever having to set foot in a courtroom. An attorney who is comfortable and eloquent around people is considered a born trial lawyer.

A writer must be both. Researching at the library and courthouse and finding needles in paperstacks is the back-room stuff of our business. There comes a time, though, when that mound of records and information is as lifeless as a petrified tree. And that's when you need people.

5

THE HUMAN FACTOR: SOURCES AND INTERVIEWS

The most famous source in American journalism was Deep Throat, a mysterious person who hung around subterranean garages at night giving snippets of information to a *Washington Post* reporter. Deep Throat helped topple a U.S. President, won a Pulitzer Prize for the *Washington Post,* and made lots of money for two reporters—proving, I think, the ultimate power of the interview.

One veteran editor of mine used to prowl through the news room reminding anyone who would listen: "In this business, you're only as good as your sources." Upon time and reflection, I must agree entirely with him, adding only that the ability to *find* sources is equally important. None of us, after all, arrives on this planet with a list of sources. Any writer of prose—fiction or nonfiction—will at one time or another need to get information about something from a knowledgeable person. That person is called a *source.* The ability to talk to your source and get the information you need is called *interviewing*.

You should keep in mind some basic ground rules of interviewing. First, it is essential to make sure that your sources know what they're talking about. Beware—some people might pretend to know something just to get their names in print or have lunch bought for them or have their egos stroked. I put my sources through a test that tells me if they know what they're talking about, and importantly, if they're telling the truth. During an interview, I ask several questions to which I already know the answers. If the source tells me something different, I know he is either lying or misinformed. Whichever the case, not passing those test questions will impugn the rest of what I hear from that source.

Second, it's best that your sources don't have a grudge against your subject. At least, that's the ideal situation. In the real world, grudges do exist and people who carry them are often the most willing interview subjects. In fact, it's one of the reasons someone might take the time to talk to you. People have different reasons for talking to a writer—ego, concern, revenge, altruism, self-promotion. In each case, try to understand why the source is speaking to you. If he has a motive to shade what he says—maybe you're interviewing him about his ex-spouse, for example—make sure he speaks strictly to the facts, and later double-check statements for accuracy. (Yes, I've interviewed my share of ex-spouses. Obviously, they know lots of personal details and often are anxious to tell revealing secrets. But I'm always careful to back up what they say with other sources and documented material.)

With stories that have a potential for legal difficulties, double sources are a must. It is easy for one person to be inaccurate or untruthful (and there are times you don't know the answer and therefore can't be sure about the source's veracity), but if a second person tells you the same thing in a separate interview, you are on firmer ground. Don't start off saying to Source #2: "Source #1 tells me this and this. Is that true?" Ask your questions as if you had not talked to anyone else, then compare the answers. Wait until your new source has finished volunteering information before you start double-checking another source's information. Remember, one of the most important follow-up questions is always: "*How* do you know this?" Make a source help you document his information. Usually, someone won't say, "I know this is true because my foot is itching." He will say he saw it happen (eyewitness is the best back-up) or heard it or read it somewhere. In the case of the latter two, you will have to find the original source; otherwise, you are stuck with hearsay information, which is not strong or verifiable.

Following are some other important tips that will help you obtain valuable and accurate information from an interview:

- *For sit-down interviews, prepare a list of question areas. The first question you ask is the most important because it will set the tone. Don't ask the toughest questions first; save them for near the end.*
- *Avoid questions that can be answered "Yes" and "No." Instead, ask questions that begin, "How do you feel about..." and "Can you describe for me...".*
- *Do your homework first. It is a waste of time, and can be insulting to the person you're interviewing, to ask questions you could have answered yourself by doing some advance preparation.*
- *Establish your relationship with the interviewee. Let him know who you are, the purpose of your interview, what you are planning to write, what you have done before. Give him a reason to cooperate, such as a dislike for injustice or a sense of fair play.*
- *Hide your surprise at revealing information. Treat it casually so they won't clam up and think, "Oh, my God, what did I say?"*
- *Use your ignorance wisely. A vulnerable interviewer who says, "Can you explain that to me?" is an irresistible student. Let the person you're interviewing be your teacher.*
- *Challenge the interviewee when necessary. When you ask questions that start with "Some critics say that..." and "Your opponents say that..." and "It has been reported that..." and "Let's play devil's advocate for a moment..." the tough questions don't seem to originate with you. The person you're interviewing will be more likely to keep talking.*
- *After a sensitive question and answer, allow for a pause. Sometimes, afterthoughts are your best material. Smile, shake your head, wait five or ten seconds.*

When it comes to defending yourself in court, named sources

are always preferable to the infamous anonymous source. Better still are named sources who will show up in court as your witnesses and repeat, in front of the judge and jury, what they told you. Of course, certain sources are going to be more believable than others. The ex-con with a knife scar across his forehead will not be believed as easily as the clean-cut businessman in a suit. Be prudent in your selection and use of certain individuals as sources. (Don't get me wrong; I've certainly used ex-cons as sources. It's just that when doing so, I make a special effort to get backup or documentation about what they tell me.)

Much has been written about a journalist's responsibility to protect confidential sources. Promising to keep a source's identity confidential is a heavy burden and not one you should assume unless there is no way to avoid it. If it takes a little more work and a few additional interviews to get the same information from named sources, by all means do the extra work.

Granting confidentiality to a source means you will tell *no one*—including your editor—the identity of that person. If a lawsuit results, the writer is sometimes protected from divulging the source under Constitutional safeguards. However, when the editor is called to the stand and questioned, he may have no such protection, since he didn't make any arrangement of confidentiality with the source.

Some editors have become increasingly cautious about such situations, especially following the Janet Cooke debacle at the *Washington Post* some years back. The same newspaper that brought us Deep Throat published an award-winning article by Cooke that was based on fabricated sources. Cooke's editors (ironically, one of them was Watergate reporter Bob Woodward) reportedly had asked the identity of Cooke's source, but when she refused on grounds of confidentiality, they published the article anyway. When the truth came out that Cooke had made up her key source, the Pulitzer Prize that had been awarded her and the paper was revoked.

Nowadays, if you decline to reveal a source to an editor, it's possible that you won't be able to use that source's information in your article. Some editors will allow exceptions when they know you and have worked with you in the past. Also, trusting editors will sometimes ask you to tell them *about* your source without revealing his name. Has he worked in the same company as your subject? Is she an ex-business partner? An old friend? Enemy? *Why* is this source's information to be believed?

Some courts have ruled in libel cases that writers must either name their sources or accept the legal presumption that there is no such source. Given that choice, it can come down to naming a source or losing the lawsuit. (Some libel insurance policies carried by publishers are invalid if a writer declines to name a source.) That's why writing organizations throughout the country have become more cautious about the use of confidential sources. The *Columbia Journalism Review* quotes one publication lawyer as follows: "Now we try to reach an understanding with sources about how we will and won't protect them. . . . (If) it turns out that the source is wrong or lying, we've got to be able to reveal the name in a deposition or maybe even depose the source ourselves."

When you find yourself in a dilemma because of information provided by a confidential source—perhaps you're losing sections of your manuscript, or maybe even about to have an article killed—it's good to go back to your source and ask for help. Sometimes you might get it. Possibly there are portions of your story in which the source will agree to be named. Perhaps the source's main worry is really about only one quote that isn't important to you. So, you can drop that quote and use her as an attributed source for the rest of the information.

There are several types of sources:

● *Named sources.* These are the best, particularly when they go "all the way to the courthouse" with you. When a quote is attributed to a real, live person, it is more believable. And it is more legally defensible.

● *Not for attribution.* You can use what was said, in direct quotes or by paraphrasing, but you cannot name the person. Most journalists consider these *off-the-record* sources. But you must make sure when a source says, "This is off the record," that you understand each other: you should reply, "Okay, I won't use your name." Legally, these sources can sometimes pose a problem. If you are sued, you might need the source to come forward for your defense. Again, it doesn't hurt to ask. If the source refuses, though, there is no way you can give him away. A journalist who reveals a confidential source will not find many editors or publishers knocking at his door.

● *Background.* You can't use a source's name or publish any of the *information* the source gives you. Yet this type of source can be valuable. (In fact, Deep Throat was a background source.) The idea is for the source to put you on the right course, and along the way it's your job to find someone else who will confirm the information for publication—preferably someone you can quote by name.

I always make a point of attempting to "upgrade" my sources. Eventually, and ideally, I would like to turn all my sources into named sources. Sometimes it is possible to move one up the ladder a step or two—maybe from a background source to a not-for-attribution source. For example, when a source first talked to you, he might have been concerned about being the only person who agreed to tell some shocking tale and was afraid of being singled out. Later, when you have a half dozen other people giving you bits and pieces of that tale, this first confidential source might decide to join the crowd and allow you to quote him by name.

An important point: just because a source is protected by confidentiality on one point doesn't mean that everything else he tells you has to be protected. Find out what it is that concerns your source, and make your deal as narrow and defined as possible: "Okay, you don't want me to use this and I won't. Now let's go back on the record." In my notebook, I circle the appropriate information and write in the margin, "Off the record," to make sure I don't forget. Highly sensitive off-the-record comments from a confidential source should not be kept in a notebook that contains the source's name on the lead page, as your notes could be subject to a subpoena requiring you to turn them over. I make some sort of code name for my source that only I know. For instance, I've once used "Blue Hat" for a police officer who gave me off-the-record information that was critical of his boss, the chief of police.

There is such a thing as sources changing their minds and deciding they don't want to tell you something after they have already done so. Once, working on an investigation of a leading political figure, I received a telegram from a key on-the-record source a few days after I interviewed him, saying: "I withdraw everything I told you. I will deny it all. Do not quote me." How do you handle *that?*

First, understand that everything that source told me was still valid, and it would have been ethical and proper for me to use it. But I was interested in finding out *why* my source had such a change of heart. I asked him, and it turned out that he had been threatened with loss of income and possible physical harm by some friends of the powerful politician. In other words, my source had been intimidated. This repelled me, as it did my editor, who even suggested that we might want to include this in the article. (Our lawyers later rejected that notion.) Obviously, I didn't want the source to have his legs broken because of my story. But I pointed out that often the best protection *is* to be quoted in a story, that then the bad guys would think twice about bothering him because he would have the power of the press behind him. Beating up a source in a story is a good way to get *another story* published. Usually, the offended parties just want the attention to go away and won't take such a chance.

There was something else at work here, though, that could have affected my ability to legally defend my story should the politician sue me. If I ignored this source's threat and went ahead and used all of the information he gave me, I would have to do so knowing that this guy was not going to help me if I ever ended up in court being sued for libel. And he might even end up testifying against me, by denying that he told me certain things. Then it would come down to the jury's deciding which one of us to believe.

In the end, we compromised. On a few points that bothered my source, I had no intention of quoting him anyway. On others that weren't important to me, I promised not to use them. And in turn, he agreed to be quoted on some other matters that were important to me and that did appear in the story. Everyone went away happy, except the politician, who threatened to sue me but never did.

One of the more mystifying aspects of writing, especially for beginners, is knowing how to find sources. Or, to be more accurate, how to find, cultivate, and keep sources. Here are some suggestions:

● *Attend professionals' speeches and seminars.* Get the names of professional groups in your area and write them for a schedule of their upcoming events. If a topic looks interesting—either for a story or to pick up a knowledgeable source for a future story—then either attend the meeting to make arrangements to get a printed copy of the speech. There are two reasons for this: you find new sources this way, and importantly, speakers often let down their guard when they're among colleagues, either saying something that is eminently quotable or at least being easier to approach.

● *Remember the ordinary people, too.* Barbers, cabbies, secretaries, court reporters, beat policemen, and other people in relatively unglamorous jobs often observe and hear influential people at their most vulnerable. These sources usually don't talk to reporters simply because they are so seldom asked. Be sure to make an effort: take them out to lunch, *notice* them—you might end up with a loyal and effective source for life.

- *Speak the source's language.* You will get much more respect if you've done your homework ahead of time and know the difference, for example, between a pretrial hearing and preliminary hearing before talking to a lawyer. Elite professionals—I sometimes refer to them as professional elitists—will quickly dismiss someone who doesn't at least make an effort to speak their language.

- *Police, prosecutors, and defense lawyers.* Everyone tries to talk to them before or during trial, when they really can't say much. Try seeking them out after the courtroom antics are over, when the heat is off. Get them to analyze the trial, to let you know what went on behind the scenes. Even if you don't do a story this time, you will have learned something—and possibly gained a source that you'll be able to use some other time.

- *Just listen.* Periodically talk to your sources when you don't need them, when there's no pressure or story deadline. This makes them feel appreciated, and it is a good way to learn more about these people so that when the time comes, you will have the necessary rapport with them.

With untrusted sources, refrain from trying to impress them with everything you know about a subject. Remember, the interviewee is supposed to be doing most of the talking, not you. Police are trained to act unimpressed with informants so that the source will keep producing information. Stop the interview if your source is giving you nothing.

Some sources will say they want to see what you're going to write before it goes into print. For me and most publications I've written for, this is a major no-no. Under no circumstances do I allow anyone the right of review. Even someone I am profiling in a major story is not allowed to read and approve my work. My feeling is that the magazine or publisher has hired me, not a committee made up of various people who are named in the story, to write the article or book. Satisfying your editors and the readers is your primary duty.

You'll have to accept the fact that not everyone you write a story about will like what you say. That's okay—I would much rather my editors and the readers like what I write.

What you can do, though, is promise to telephone a source or subject and read back their direct quotes that you're using. After all, these are their words; they should be able to live with them. The rest of the words are yours, and you should not allow a source or subject to tamper with them. But even this arrangement is not something I routinely do. Rather, it's a concession I make to a person who is tying his cooperation to a prepublication look at what I'm writing.

Once, one of my magazine-writing students received an assignment from a regional magazine to profile a successful businesswoman. The entrance to the businesswoman's office was guarded by a pushy public relations man who made my student promise that he could review her article before she sent it to the magazine. When she took him the article the following week, he rewrote it and sent the new version to the magazine, along with a nice cover letter. My student came into class with two articles, her original and the PR guy's version, and asked what she should do. When I came down off the ceiling, I explained that she had made a big mistake. And that the PR guy had erred badly, too.

"But he said he wouldn't let me interview her unless he could see the story," the student protested.

"And you believed him?" I asked. "Weren't you doing a positive story that would have made his boss look good?"

"Yes."

"Do you really think he would have kept you away from her? If you had turned him down, I'll bet he would have done a quick shuffle and taken you in to see her. I think you'd better call the magazine and try to save your story."

But the damage had already been done, and the magazine ended up canceling her assignment. The editor had been both offended and disgusted—offended by the PR guy's obvious attempt to manipulate the magazine's coverage of his employer and disgusted by the writer's poor judgment. In such situations, clearly there are no winners—not the writer, not the magazine, not the PR man, not the businesswoman.

Interviewing is an essential part of writing. The ability to ask questions, to listen attentively, to take accurate notes, all will determine the quality of information you'll be gathering from your writing. Here are some final suggestions:

- *Don't slander.* Be careful in the phrasing of your questions so that you won't be accused of slandering anybody. Slander, of course, is the verbal equivalent of libel. There have been a few recent lawsuits aimed at writers who have asked questions like these: "Did Mr. Smith ever steal money? Do you know if he used drugs? Do you know if he participated in wild sex parties?" If Mr. Smith is innocent of such behavior, then he could have a juicy slander suit.

- *Conduct interviews with major sources in person so you can see whom you are dealing with.* If you get sued, you will not want to see your major source for the first time on a witness stand. Maybe he has purple hair and is given to wearing red miniskirts. And if he is supposed to be an informed source on the banking industry, for example, the jury might disbelieve him—and your story as well.

- *Tape-record certain interviews.* Most magazines and some publication lawyers request copies of interview tapes, in case of any questions about the subject's comments. Of course, it is not practical to tape every interview. Having to transcribe a tape is long and tedious work. Often, I've had journalism students object to the necessity of learning how to keep accurate notes. Usually there's someone in class who'll say something like: "I'll just tape all of my interviews." Soon thereafter, I make a point of assigning a one-hour, question-and-answer interview that must be taped and *transcribed.* The students come in days later, usually with about twenty typed pages of transcription, mumbling about how much work it took. Welcome to the wonderful world of taping. So, a writer needs to be selective in taping, preserving only those interviews that are especially complex or controversial.

  State laws vary, but in California, Florida, New York, and other states (a total of thirteen at last count), it is against the law to secretly tape-record a telephone conversation. Many writers, particularly newspaper reporters, subvert the law by taping without asking for permission. But such a tape will do you little good other than to help with your note taking because you cannot present it to lawyers or the court since it was illegally obtained. (Some reporters destroy such tapes after they are sure they have everything down in their notes.)

- *Be tight lipped with sources before publication.* The military has long dispensed classified information on a "need to know" basis. Writers should do the same. One writer's careless remarks to a source that he wished someone would "rifle" the safe of the subject he was investigating ended up in a libel suit filed against the writer by the subject. "Keep quiet," John Paul Jones wrote in his respected textbook, *Gathering and Writing the News.* "An investigative reporter on a story should not talk a great deal about what he is doing. He should be tight lipped, like any other investigator handling a delicate matter. In the first place, his investigation may turn out to be fruitless. Secondly, loose talk about his progress on a case may be used against him."

Journalists are learning the hard way the importance of being tight lipped before publication. Loose talk during your researching, loaded questions asked of sources, and careless internal memos may invite libel and slander lawsuits. In one case reported by the *Columbia Journalism Review,* two Illinois reporters could have avoided a $9.2 million libel *judgment* if they had refrained from naming a local builder in a memorandum. Though the information was never published in the paper, in this case just circulating a memo constituted publication. (Their newspaper was forced into bankruptcy court and ended up paying about $1.5 million to the plaintiff.)

A final word about sources and subjects and interviews. Remember, these are people you're dealing with, not court records or published documentation found in library archives. People have feelings, and I always try to make that work in my favor by finding some way to motivate them into wanting to help me. If they have a good reason to assist you, they will spend a lot more time with you than if you are merely seen as a bother.

People are the most important sources of information for a writer. They will inevitably provide the most revealing information, the most poignant scenes. In interviewing them, be open and nonjudgmental. Once, I went into a California prison to interview a man convicted of more than 100 rapes. I had an assignment to profile this scoundrel, and my plan was to write the story in such a way that women who read it would know how this guy succeeded in finding and trapping his victims. As I sat across from him in the visiting room, I had to be open and friendly and nonjudgmental in order to get him to talk. Yet, clearly, this was not somebody I would want to invite home for dinner with my family. I think of it as taking off my personal hat and putting on my journalism hat. In short, I got the information I needed, the article was published and I hope that at least a few women learned things they might do to keep themselves from ever becoming rape victims. Another example, I think, of the power of the interview.

6

PROTECTION FOR THE FICTION WRITER

A novelist friend of mine likes to think he's immune to libel. "You write facts, I write fiction," he's fond of reminding me. In a recent discussion, it became clear that the major character in his last novel was based on a childhood playmate. The character in his book became a mass killer.

"Was your pal a mass killer?" I asked.

"Of course not," my friend replied. "But I always thought he was capable of killing."

"If you've made him too identifiable, he could sue you and win," I said, knowing that I sounded like a Beverly Hills lawyer.

"I'm not worried. The guy hasn't read a book in his life."

While my friend may have stumbled across the ultimate protection for writers everywhere—none of us would be sued if our works went unread—it's not something I'd like to encourage or count on. I want people to read my writing, and secondly, I'd like my friend and other writers of fiction to know that there are ways to safely draw material for their work from their everyday lives without becoming possible legal targets.

Throughout the modern era of publishing and until quite recently, authors have felt safe as long as they called their work fiction and began with the usual disclaimer that went something like: "Nothing you read here is true." And though courts had long agreed that fictional works *could* be libelous under the right circumstances, for a long time the verdicts favored writers.

One bygone case involved the book (and film) *Anatomy of a Murder*, a fictional account of an actual murder trial and written by the defense attorney. The wife and daughter of the real victim sued for libel, claiming that their fictional counterparts had portrayed them in an unflattering light. Indeed, though the names were changed, the characters (including physical descriptions), locale, and details of the trial could all be identified with the real people and places. Yet the court ruled against the plaintiffs on a narrow issue: the age difference between the real mother and daughter was different from that of the fictional characters. Also, the court added that anyone familiar with the upstanding plaintiffs would know that they didn't possess the unsavory aspects of the fictional characters. (In today's legal climate, the plaintiffs would surely have prevailed, and rightly so, I'm afraid.)

In another interesting case from the annals of publishing law, the *Saturday Evening Post* was sued in the late 1960s over a fictional short story about a character named Esco Brooks. The plaintiff, an old friend of the author's, thought that the character and incidents in the story were based on his life. The plaintiff's name was Larry Esco Middlebrooks. The court agreed that if a fictional character could be identified as the plaintiff, the author could be liable. But despite witnesses who testified that they thought the plaintiff and character were one and the same, the court ruled in favor of the writer, finding that differences in the ages and professions of the plaintiff and character in the story made identification unreasonable. In sympathy with writers everywhere, the court wrote: "Authors of necessity must rely on their own background and experiences in writing fiction."

In the 1970s, the legal winds began to blow in the opposite direction. One of the first casualties was best-seller novelist Gwen Davis Mitchell and her publisher, Doubleday. In Mitchell's novel, *Touching*, there was a description of a nude marathon session—a sort of psychology encounter assembly—led by a fictional character named Dr. Simon Herford. A real clinical psychologist, Paul Bindrim, who led nude marathon sessions, sued Mitchell and Doubleday. Bindrim produced a contract that Mitchell had signed before he allowed her to participate in one of the therapy sessions. The author had agreed not to disclose the names of those who attended the marathon or descriptions of what transpired during the session. Though the physical descriptions of Herford and Bindrim were quite different, and although Herford was depicted as a psychiatrist and not a psychologist, tape recordings of actual sessions conducted by Bindrim were similar to sessions portrayed in the book. The court decided that colleagues and patients could reasonably recognize Herford as Bindrim, and furthermore, found that Mitchell had exhibited actual malice by using the real session that she had attended for a scene in her novel. (Bindrim had been found to be a public figure and, yes, even in fiction, public figures must show malice in order to win libel cases.) The court ordered a $75,000 award for the psychologist—$25,000 against Doubleday and $50,000 against Mitchell.

In another sign of changing times, Doubleday turned around and sued Mitchell for the amount of the libel award plus interest and legal expenses—a total of $138,000. The publisher based its suit on the standard indemnities and warranties provision in the contract Mitchell signed, in which the author agreed to hold Doubleday harmless from any claim, suit, or action, and any resulting expenses or damages. The publisher was especially piqued because Mitchell had reportedly assured her editors before publication that the characters in her book were completely fictional. (Doubleday's suit was controversial and unpopular among writers, and eventually it was settled out of court.)

As a result of the Bindrim case, agents and authors found that novels that appeared too similar to real-life people and events were rejected by worried publishers. Completed manuscripts were more closely scrutinized by publishing houses and their attorneys, and authors were questioned in detail about the sources of their inspiration.

Writers of fiction should remember an important rule: *Before a plaintiff can begin to prove defamation, it must be shown that "a reasonable person would understand that the fictional character was, in actual fact, the plaintiff."* If a writer has used a little creativity in changing some basic characteristics and events—and *not* signed a contract with a source promising to exclude information that is later used—it should, in most cases, be sufficient to keep a plaintiff from proving "reasonable identification."

Fiction writers can help protect themselves against lawsuits by making sure they use names that have no resemblance to real people. It is essential to check phone books and other records in the locale of the fictional story to make sure there isn't a real person with the same name as your made-up character. Also, make sure either by taking a research trip to the area or by checking through the local Chamber of Commerce that there's no business of the type described in a novel at or near the location where it's said to be in the book. Of course, short of combing through every phone book in the country, nothing will guard against the accidental or coincidental use of a name of *somebody somewhere.* But if you pull the name James Smithson off the top of your head, as I'm doing here, and have him frolicking through your fiction as a crazed psychiatrist from Cleveland, it's a darn good idea to check the Cleveland phone book for just such a person. And if you find one, to change the name to James Whatever—as long as there isn't anyone by *that* name.

Even after a plaintiff has proved identification in a suit against a work of fiction, the case is far from over. The plaintiff must prove that the average reader would believe the defamatory statements in the work to be factual. A fictional short story in *Penthouse* about a baton-twirling Miss Wyoming who performed fellatio on her coach at the Miss America pageant—causing him to levitate—was the target of a lawsuit by a woman who was a former Miss Wyoming and whose talent in the Miss America contest was baton twirling. Though the trial jury awarded her $26 million in damages, an appellate court reduced the amount to zero. The high court found that the story could not "reasonably be understood as describing actual facts."

In addition to libel and invasion of privacy, charges of pornography or obscenity can be a real headache to a fiction writer. Current law offers no absolute guidelines, not even that of "literary merit" or "redeeming social worth." Local "community" standards determine what's obscene; and what's considered just lively adult entertainment in Las Vegas may be the target of a lawsuit for "pandering obscenity" in Forth Worth or Cincinnati.

Not only are there a variety of local "community" standards which a given national publication may find itself in conflict with, but a writer who doesn't know and adhere to the industry's own standards may find his manuscript unpublishable because of the steamy passage on page 102. So, in writing, as in romance, it's wise to know what you're getting into and how far you're prepared to go.

A case in point: Though I usually don't admit this in mixed company, early on in my writing career I once tried to infiltrate the adult-book market. As I recall, those publishers were paying $1,500 per manuscript for stuff that seemed a cinch to write once you figured out the formula. After mailing in my manuscript, I received a letter back from an editor congratulating me on my writing abilities but reminding me that I was writing for a "masturbating readership." He told me I needed to be much more explicit and gave me a list of "must" words to include—the kind of words usually found on the walls of public restrooms. I "dirtied up" the manuscript and sent it back for another go. A few weeks later, I received a letter from another editor, advising me that the first editor was no longer working there. She said something about my being a good writer, then added, "But your manuscript is much too pornographic." For years I had those two letters, framed, in my office.

The lesson here is that even among editors at the same adult-book publisher, there's a difference of opinion as to what's pornographic and what's not.

(Note to my mother: I never did make a sale to this market.)

If you're aiming at mass-market magazines that aren't specifically sexually oriented, read a few issues and see how much explicitness seems the rule. If you're hoping to sell to a commercial trade book publisher, look it up in *Writer's Market* and see if any information has been offered on restrictions on, or requirements for, adult material in their publications. Many romance publishers helpfully offer guidelines on what's appropriate for each of their lines of romances—how much sex is obligatory and how much, or what kind, is prohibited.

Things are more liberal among commercial trade publishers, by the way, since the major book clubs started adding "X" ratings in advertising books with explicit sex or language, rather than refusing to carry such books at all for fear of offending their readership. And as a result, publishers are more willing to publish books with strong and/or explicit sexual content, since such books aren't automatically unsalable or lawsuit targets, as they would have been twenty or thirty years ago.

Generally speaking, some markets refuse sex altogether—

publications on religion, and those whose primary readership is children or teenagers, for example. Current mainstream magazines allow sex, but not the sort of play-by-play details that book publishers find acceptable. The steamier romance series and men's/women's magazines (the sort that carry ads for sexual implements) allow detail, but not the more extreme perversions. And in the publications that come in brown paper wrappers, I'm told, almost anything goes that's not actually illegal—to do or to portray. That's obscene in all territories, for all markets.

So unless you're aiming at specifically adult markets, if your tale contains some scenes you'd be embarrassed to read aloud before a group of strangers, ask yourself: what do current industry standards permit, where this piece might be published? Will my piece show up on the editor's desk with a strike against it from the beginning? Am I willing to risk that? Am I willing to have the book or story stand or fall by these scenes—are they that important to what I want to say? If, in your judgment, your scenes *are* important, and if you think you can find an appropriate market for the piece, then go ahead. Many contemporary best sellers seldom leave the bedroom, and yours may turn out to be the next one.

A writer must also be aware of a whole new set of problems arising from *fictionalization* or *faction*—presenting fact as fiction or fiction as fact. While factual characters can lend authenticity to your fiction writing, there is obvious risk involved in taking such literary liberties, even if the people named are public figures. Warren Spahn, the former baseball star, sued the publisher of *The Warren Spahn Story*, a nonfiction young-adult biography in which the author fictionalized dialogue and attributed thoughts and feelings to Spahn that had no basis in reality or in the author's research. Misstating and misconstruing such personal events in Spahn's life as his childhood, his relationship with his father, the courtship of his wife, his marriage, and his military experience constituted "material and substantial falsification," in the court's words, which translated to *actual malice* and resulted in Spahn's winning his case.

The author of a fictional manuscript is the first and foremost authority on whether there exists a potential for legal difficulties. Editors decide whether or not to send works out for legal review (called *vetting*), and unlike writers, they have no way of knowing when a problem lurks between the lines. If my friend's editor had asked him if his mass killer was based on a real person, I'm sure he would have said, "Of course not." And he wouldn't have been lying, because he genuinely felt (and feels) that this killer was a fictional character he had made up in his own literary fantasies. Many fictional characters are, of course, composites of numerous people the authors have known and loved and hated. The very essence of our craft is writing about something we *know*. Therein lies the conflict in fiction writing.

Writers of fiction should carefully examine the basis for their ideas and characters. If you've used someone in your life as a model for a character in a novel, disguise that character enough so that the real counterpart will not have a case. Make the names and descriptions dissimilar—even change someone's race or gender. And, of course, include a strong disclaimer. If you think a problem might develop, talk to your editor openly and honestly. A publishing house and its lawyers are happy to work with you at this point, and they would much rather identify and resolve a problem before publication than be surprised later on in a court of law.

7

WRITING AND EDITING TIPS

When should you stop researching and start writing? Only after you've *over-researched* your topic. Writing is very much the business of selecting the best material and leaving the rest behind. I can always tell when I've researched enough. I have a feeling that my cup runneth over—I have all the written documents I need, sources start telling me things I've already heard, and I've started to write in my mind's eye, maybe when I'm in the shower or seated at the dinner table. That's the time to put the blank paper in the typewriter, or in my case, turn on the computer and face an empty screen. The emptiness will not last for long. The magic is about to begin.

Just make sure it's not the stuff of hocus-pocus. Don't get caught up in the fun of writing purple prose and start filling in holes in your research with things you wish were true. Sure, even in the best nonfiction it would sometimes make a better story if events didn't happen quite the way they did. But when you write nonfiction, you tell *the truth*. And in case of a lawsuit, the truth is your first and best defense. So, if you aren't sure of the accuracy of a particular fact or quote, *don't use it.* That way, it can never be used against you in a future lawsuit.

While you need to pick and choose quotes to reflect the angle of your story or scene, remember:

- *Direct quotes must be strong.* Quoting a person highlights those words, so they must be important and eloquent. If they aren't smashing, then paraphrase. For instance, I would not quote someone saying, "I was born in New Orleans." That is not the sort of information that needs to go in quotes. I can say that myself at the appropriate place. Better to save your quotes for something like: "I grew up playing on the Mississippi. My childhood was like a Mark Twain tale."

- *Never put words into someone's mouth.* When you put quotation marks on either side of a statement, it is sacrosanct. Those words and the meaning of them belong not to you but to the person who is quoted. If you did not get the quote you think you need, then no amount of tinkering will fix it. You must go back to your source for more interviewing. The following scenario touches on a potential trouble spot.

Writer: "When you heard about the bankruptcy of ABC Computers, did you feel cheated and upset?"

Subject: "Yeah."

If in your manuscript you write, "Joe Blow said, 'When I heard about the bankruptcy of ABC Computers, I felt cheated and upset,'" you have put words into Blow's mouth. I admit that this sort of thing does happen, especially by newspaper reporters, who don't have time to work a better quote out of a person. But some editors will fire a writer who gets caught doing this. And if you get sued because of a potentially libelous statement solicited in this manner, you could be in trouble. A better way to deal with the recalcitrant Joe Blow would be to paraphrase, writing something like: "Blow admitted to feeling cheated and upset."

- *When paraphrasing, you must still be accurate.* Paraphrasing does not relieve a writer of the responsibility to accurately reflect someone's opinion or position. Just because you don't use quotation marks doesn't mean that you have the freedom to misstate what someone said or meant.

- *In reconstructed dialogue, it's best to talk to all participants.* Say you are reconstructing a conversation between a businesswoman and her partner. In that case, you should talk to both parties. But if the second person is dead or unavailable or unnamed, you can use the businesswoman's rendition of the conversation as long as you tell the reader that's what you're doing.

- *Always identify the source of quotes.* Let there be no confusion about who said what. This can be a problem when there is more than one person speaking and the writer favors "she said" and "he said."

- *Practice utmost care in editing quotes.* Certainly, you are free to use parts of a quote and leave out unnecessary words. And you may do so in most cases without ellipses (. . .), the constant use of which would become unwieldy whenever a writer left out a word or a sentence. And how about changing a few words here and there in a quote? This is a difficult point to make, and I always seem to get into trouble whenever I try to explain it to a class of eager-beaver young journalists. An editor once described it to me like this: "There's the school of actual quote and the school of literal quotes. We prefer the latter." And so does every publication for which I've ever written. So the answer is a surprising *yes* to the question can you change a few words.

However, the following caution is italicized for a reason: *Your editing must never change the meaning of a quotation.* The most common allowable changes are ones of grammar, syntax, and tone. I will always change, "I ain't talked to him," to: "I haven't talked to him." But if someone tells me he had his feelings "hurt," I will not change it to "devastated." Also, often in conversation, a person will stop in the middle of a sentence for an aside, then finish the original sentence a minute or two later. A writer can correctly and ethically bring that sentence together in print, as it was meant to be, without being accused of misquoting.

- *Guard against out-of-context quotes.* The most common mistake made in this area is having a person answering a question in print that is different from the one that was actually posed during the interview. Television news is often accused of doing this, and sometimes with justification. Keeping accurate notes will guard against inadvertent mistakes of this kind. If you're frustrated by a source's inept answer to a key question, then ask it again, and keep asking it until the words come together more eloquently. Often, when I've found myself stuck with an inelegant quote when I'm busy writing, I've picked up the phone and asked my source: "Could you say that in a different way?"

The best nonfiction these days reads like fiction; it is full of dramatic scenes, well-crafted dialogue, and people's unspoken thoughts. In nonfiction, though, you must avoid reporting a source's thoughts unless the source tells you exactly what he was thinking at a particular time. There are exceptions, such as the piece I wrote for *Esquire* on the convicted embezzler, who did not allow me to interview him. Without access to him, how could I possibly know what he was thinking? My story would have been one-dimensional if I had not come across a gold mine: federal court transcripts that contained everything I needed, including the felon's thoughts at crucial times. When the subject went before a federal judge for sentencing, the judge took him over every step of the crime from beginning to end, asking such questions as, "What were you *thinking* as you walked through customs with the diamonds in your suitcase?" Much to my delight, this sort of detailed questioning went on for nearly 100 pages and provided the unspoken thoughts I needed for my story.

Unauthorized biographies can pose a particular problem for a writer. In such a project, the writer seldom gets the opportunity to interview the subject—otherwise it would undoubtedly be called an authorized work. So, the challenge is to find friends and associates who can report on the subject from firsthand experience and provide the details necessary to reconstruct scenes. A major requirement, though, is that the source was actually present in the scene or event you are recreating, as using hearsay might open you to a lawsuit from the subject. Authorized biographies, in which you find yourself with complete access to the subject's actions and thoughts, are much different (and easier).

Whether you're writing nonfiction or fiction, organization is crucial. Make sure all your research material is close at hand. Before writing, I sift through all my notes and accumulated information one last time. I make two stacks, one containing valuable stuff I know I'll use, and the other, not-so-valuable material that I don't think I'll need. What statistics am I going to use? Who are the sources and subjects I'm going to use to support my theme? And which quotes? I jot down my ideas on what I want to be sure to include. In this way, I start deciding what structure my piece is going to take. What chronology of events will work best? This is as close as I get to writing an outline. Some writers go to great lengths to construct a detailed, blow-by-blow outline before they start writing. Myself, I'm always too anxious at this point to start writing, and I don't want to use up my creative juices on an outline. There are no rules on whether you should or shouldn't make an outline; whatever suits you best is fine, as long as it works.

Interestingly, most mistakes that go into print are made in the first draft. So, take the time before you start writing or as you go along to look up proper spelling, correct names, and accurate quotations. It is tempting to say to yourself, "I'll check that later." But I've found that later, I almost never remember what it was that I was supposed to check unless I've done so at the time or made a big note to myself.

Most magazine pieces are written in the third-person and have a strong point of view. Like your theme, the point of view of your article must remain consistent throughout or you will confuse the reader. For instance, a piece I wrote for *Playboy* (Today's Navy—Not a Job, an Adventure," August 1983) was all about the mysterious death aboard ship of a young sailor and the lies and cover-ups concocted by the Navy in not telling the sailor's father the truth about his son's death. My point of view was one of outrage, like the father's—outrage at the Navy for allowing a situation that caused a young man's death to exist aboard ship, and outrage at the Navy for not leveling with the father. I did not attempt to tell the Navy's side of the story, though I did ask for interviews with the Secretary of the Navy and others on down, including the captain of the ship, but received no cooperation. My article told primarily the story of the dead boy and his father. But when I took on the Navy, I had more than just the father's word—I had legally-supportable backup, most notably a long report by a military investigative agency that criticized the Navy's handling of the case. (I got a copy of this report from the father's attorney, who had filed a wrongful death suit against the Navy.) In the heat of writing, you need to remember that satisfactory backup is almost always required by editors and publishers. I could not, for example, have said that the boy was murdered—even though ill-treatment hastened his death from "sun stroke"—because no one was tried and convicted of murder. Remember, semantics is a writer's business.

Writers work at different paces. One writer I know feels he has had a successful day if he's written fifty words. My quota is 1,000 words a day. (When my goal is reached, I stick on my calendar for that day a gold star like your elementary school teacher used to put on your best papers. My family has learned to steer clear of me until I have my gold star for the day.)

However slowly or quickly you write, you should always allow for a cooling-off period after the first draft. I make a point of putting the manuscript aside for a day or two, even a week, in order to overcome my enthusiasm for my own brilliance. Then I go back to it, reconsidering everything, editing it coolly and unmercifully. Only after I do a final bulletproofing—checking all quotes, making sure of my sources, and so forth—is my writing ready for others' eyes.

After your manuscript goes in to the magazine or book publisher, the editor goes over it before anyone else does. More editors these days are sensitive to legal issues, and they may voice some cautionary notes even before any official legal review takes place. But generally, at this stage, the editor is reading your work for content and style. Occasionally, you will be hit for what I call an "editorial rewrite," meaning that the requested changes have nothing to do with legalities, but rather with such mundane things as clarity of writing. If an editor questions the lucidity or clarity of anything at all, he or she is completely correct by definition. If what you're saying is not understood, then you have failed to communicate your meaning. In these cases, you may disagree with suggestions the editor has for fixing the troublesome area, but you should not argue that something is clear to you and therefore must be clear to all.

Editing is a collaborative venture in which the editor and the writer work together. But there is a place where you must draw the line. Now hear this: Don't write something that is not true just because the editor thinks it will make a stronger story. I once had a magazine editor rewrite dialogue in my manuscript. "It would be much better if he said this," the editor said. "But he didn't say that and this is nonfiction," I argued. The editor may want a particular feel to the story, but the writer's *first* responsibility must be to the story and the truth of same. You know your story better than anyone else—don't budge on factual points. There are ways, of course, to improve stories through good editing; tightening the narrative and smoothing a transition are the sort of refinements editors should make. Making up dialogue is not.

I consider my editor to be my working partner at the magazine or publishing house. After all, even though you've finished your writing, your job is far from over and the editor's is just beginning.

8

COPYRIGHT, PERMISSIONS, AND RELEASES

Under current federal copyright law, an *inherent* or *automatic* copyright happens at the moment a work is created. As long as you have not transferred the copyright, you have the right to defend your ownership and seek damages if your work is unfairly used.

You can get additional legal protection by filling out a Form TX and sending a copy of your manuscript (published or unpublished) along with ten dollars to: Register of Copyrights, Library of Congress, Washington D.C., 20559. You will receive a certificate of copyright by return mail. You must register a published work within three months of publication in order to be able to sue an infringer for punitive damages. Under the automatic copyright, you may sue only for real damages, which represent what you would have been paid. For example, if an encyclopedia publisher that normally pays $100 to contributors infringed my work, I could be awarded only $100 in real damages. Punitive damages, those meant to punish the infringer, can go into millions of dollars.

It is unnecessary to gain permission to use literary material that is not protected by copyright laws. For example, anything published before this century that has not since been copyrighted is not protected by U.S. laws and could be freely adapted. In fact, under today's laws, if such material was never published, whoever could establish legal ownership could copyright it. If you are unsure whether the material you are dealing with is protected by copyright, the Library of Congress has a fee-paid search service. They can track down a copyrighted work by author, claimant, and in some cases, title. (There is no subject search.) Write to: Reference Search Section, U.S. Copyright Office, Library of Congress, Washington D.C. 20559.

Of course, if you know something has been published, it's much easier to find out the name of the copyright holder by contacting the publisher. Usually the author of the work holds copyright, but sometimes the publisher has retained all rights. In any case, make sure you're dealing with the actual copyright holder when seeking permission. If you can't locate the copyright holder but the material is absolutely essential, you and your publisher can, as a last resort, have added to your book's permission page a notice something like this: "Attempts to contact the copyright holder for "Itching—Causes and Cures" by Ima Doctor, which appeared in the May 1952 issue of *Skin Today*, have been unsuccessful."

But remember, if the copyright holder later comes forward, you'll undoubtedly still have to pay for using the material. (Be sure to keep all records and letters regarding your attempts to trace the copyright holder so you can prove, if necessary, that you made a real, honest effort to locate him or her.)

A sample request for permission to reprint might take something like this format:

Date, 1986

Permissions Manager
XYZ Press
1220 Mound Avenue
Orafumbula, FL 12345

Dear Permissions Manager:

I am preparing a book, How to Bulletproof Your Manuscript, *to be published in Fall 1986 by Writer's Digest Books. The publisher estimates first printing as X,000 copies and the retail price as $9.95.*

I'd like nonexclusive world rights to reproduce, in my book, (specific material—title, date of publication, where published, etc. If it's an excerpt, identify the excerpt—usually by means of a photocopy).

If this is satisfactory, please sign and date this letter, specifying any wording you wish to appear as the acknowledgment, and return the letter in the enclosed envelope.

If you do not control these rights, I would appreciate your directing me to the copyright holder; if you have any questions you'd like answered before granting permission, please let me know.

Sincerely,

Bruce B. Henderson

Name _____ *Date* _____

Wording of permission _____

_____

_____

If you're not sure whether you need to get permission, refer to Chapter 4, pp. 33-34, for guidelines on fair use.

The following cardinal rule may help you avoid confusion on what you can and cannot protect under copyright law: *Ideas are not protected, but the adaption of those ideas is protected.* For instance, a copyrighted story of a young girl's heart-transplant operation in the morning newspaper may not be read aloud on the air by a television newsman later in the day. However, the news event itself is a fact and cannot be copyrighted. Television producers, upon reading about the operation in the paper, are free to send to the hospital their own crew of reporters and cameramen to create a copyrighted story of their own. (And that, of course, is what television stations—even networks—do all the time.)

To my knowledge, my copyright has been infringed only once. (I guess I have to say "allegedly" because the matter never went to court.) Without naming names, my "Love Bandits" magazine article (which I *did* register with the Copyright Office within three months of publication) was used as the basis for an hour-long episode by a popular TV cop show. I called the studio, and the producer said, "One of our writers came in with the script and we thought it was an original story. Then, just a few days ago, someone showed me your magazine article and I knew there was a problem. I suppose you're calling about a legal settlement?" The TV scriptwriter had not interviewed any of the participants in my story, and there were no other clips or articles on the sordid affair other than my *copyrighted* story. It was much more than just getting the idea for the script from my story: more than a dozen *manners of expression* were adapted for the screen directly from my article.

I called the scriptwriter, and he said, "That was a very good story you wrote. I hope you don't feel like you were ripped off. But I can see why you might." A week later, the scriptwriter was fired from the show, along with his immediate supervisor.

By then, the matter was in the hands of the law firm that represented the insurance company that covered the studio for such indiscretions. My lawyer wrote some letters, their lawyers wrote some letters, and many months later, I dropped my plans to sue when I realized how much it was going to cost me to get into federal court with my copyright infringement case. "They're playing hard ball with us," my lawyer said. "They won't settle." Before leaving my lawyer's office, I asked him to guess how much the law firm representing the studio had already billed the insurance carrier for their work on the case. "Probably twenty thousand dollars," he said. The infuriating thing was that if the producer had called when he realized there was a problem, I would have been delighted to have sold him TV rights to the story for the Writers' Guild minimum ($5,000) and a "story by" credit for the episode. But he didn't make that call and I'll never understand why. It taught me an unfortunate lesson: Sometimes a writer can do everything right in terms of copyright protection and still not win.

Legal experts favor written agreements. Of course, many civil lawyers spend their careers looking for reasons to nullify signed documents when it benefits their clients. And judges think nothing of throwing out contracts deemed to have been negotiated in bad faith. So, just because you have a signed agreement doesn't mean you're safe.

There are certain permissions and releases that may help a writer avoid a lawsuit, but I offer no guarantees. In fact, if you managed to convince the subject of an exposé to sign a prepublication agreement that said, "I promise not to sue," it would be as useful as a round-trip ticket to Mars. None of us can sign away our constitutional right to sue. (Just look at all the medical malpractice lawsuits that are filed *after* a patient has signed a release form that would appear to protect the hospital, doctors, and nurses from any type of legal action.)

One libel-prevention tactic used these days by writers and publications is to persuade sources, particularly confidential ones, to sign *affidavits*. These written statements, signed and duly witnessed by a notary public, contain all the factual information that a source has revealed to a writer. This would prevent a source from having a change of heart or otherwise failing to recall what he told the writer if the matter ever were to end up in a court of law.

In the case of a confidential source, the writer usually agrees that an affidavit would be made public in the event that there is a lawsuit *or* that it comes out that the source was inaccurate or untruthful. In having such a condition placed on the pledge of confidentiality, even a truthful and honest source would have to accept that the writer would reveal the source's identity before losing a libel lawsuit.

An underlying intent of affidavits is to keep potential plaintiffs from filing suit when they find out that such written statements exist and can be brought forward at an appropriate time. In recent years, some plaintiffs' lawyers have been accused of targeting for legal action stories and books that rely on confidential sources because they are so difficult for media organizations to defend against. "We stand by this story as being truthful but can't tell you why because we must protect our confidential source," is a defense that doesn't always impress a judge or jury. It is not unknown for plaintiffs' attorneys to file lawsuits designed to gain what they hope will be a quick and lucrative settlement without ever having to go to court. Indeed, settling a libel suit can sometimes be less expensive for a publisher than paying legal fees to win one, particularly when the need to keep a source confidential is a cornerstone of the publisher's defense.

In another type of written agreement, writers often find themselves negotiating contracts with subjects for the purpose of sharing in literary profits. Before going any further, allow me to draw a clear distinction between *sources* and *subjects*. You get information from a source; you tell a subject's story.

I can't remember ever paying a source for information in connection with a newspaper or magazine article, unless you count buying drinks and lunch for them. On the other hand, book authors regularly compensate major sources with either a flat payment or a percentage of royalties. For instance, I gave 10 percent of my royalties to a former World War II pilot who helped me with relevant facts and figures for a novel and wrote a foreword to my book. In another book project, I gave an innocent participant in a bank scandal 3 percent of my royalties. The reason I paid these sources is that they spent many hours working with me, and without their efforts I would have had to spend much more time completing the projects.

Writers occasionally enter into prepublication agreements with *subjects* of magazine pieces. Such agreements are not to share in the magazine revenue (it's inevitably too small to split) but to participate in any big money, such as book and film offers, that might result from publication of the article. These agreements can be to the advantage of the writer. If I help make someone famous by writing a story about him in a national magazine, for example, I certainly would like the option of being part of a bigger writing project that results from the exposure.

A writer I know had an idea a few years ago to profile a middle-aged surfer, sort of a grown-up Beach Boy. From the window of his southern California beach home, he watched a lot of people hit the surf every morning. He found an aging surfer, got a magazine assignment, and did the story. When the magazine came out, a producer went down to the beach and signed an agreement with the surfer to make a movie out of his story, completely bypassing the writer, who realized too late his mistake in not signing an agreement with the surfer prior to publication. "If the guy hadn't gone for it," I said, "you could have found another aging surfer to profile." But by then, it was all water under the pier.

Agreements with book coauthors are referred to as collaboration agreements. Usually a writer collaborates with a subject who has a story to tell but needs a writer to do the telling. Sometimes, one writer will collaborate with another writer. It's vital in collaboration agreements to define specific areas of responsibility so there will be no hard feelings or lawsuits later on. Take this example from a collaboration agreement of mine with the subject of a book:

> *It is understood and agreed that Henderson shall prepare a proposal and outline for the work, and that (the subject) shall cooperate with, and assist, Henderson in that preparation by meeting with Henderson and furnishing all necessary information regarding the content of the work.*

Some other points regarding collaborations:

- The writer should retain the copyright to the work. But in the event a shared copyright is necessary, there should be a clause inserted that will allow either party to file a copyright-infringement lawsuit. A writer must always be in the position to aggressively defend a copyrighted work. A clause like the following will work:

> In cases of alleged infringement of said copyright, either party may sue individually if the other party declines to join in such a suit. In the instance of either (the writer) or (the subject) suing individually, the plaintiff alone will incur all legal costs and recover all damages. If one party elects not to be named in a suit but pays half of all incurred legal costs, both parties shall share equally in any recovery of damages after legal costs and expenses.

- Since writers have to indemnify publishers, it is only fair for subjects to indemnify writers. After all, you are counting on your subject to provide truthful and accurate information. This does not protect the writer from ever being sued, however. But it does show the good intent of the writer—in case a judge and jury are looking— and it allows a mechanism for the writer to countersue an untruthful source. Such an indemnification should read as follows:

> (The subject) agrees to indemnify (the writer) and hold him harmless against any claim, demand, suit, action, proceeding, or expense of any kind arising from or based upon matter in the work that was provided by (the subject).

- Always make sure you write the agreement or have your agent (or lawyer) do so. An agreement tends to favor the person who wrote it. Better to start with what you want than have to keep picking away at someone else's version of what they want.

- A professional writer should not agree to write a book, or even a proposal for one, without being paid. In most cases, the subject should pay the writer for preparing an outline and sample chapter, both of which are necessary in order to approach publishers. The subject should be reimbursed only *after* a publishing contract has been signed and an advance against royalties paid.

- The question of how an advance should be split can be a

touchy one, but I believe the writer should get the biggest part of it. Depending on how much time a writer will be spending on the book, his share of the advance should range from 50 percent to 90 percent. The extra money a writer receives at this stage can be recouped later by the subject out of royalties, *if* the book does well enough to pay back its advance. (I've seen statistics that suggest that some 90 percent of the books published in the United States do not make back their advances.) Remember, the idea of an advance is to pay the writer for the time it takes to write a book. Subjects can often keep full-time jobs while supplying information to a writer for a book, while working on a book *is* a full-time job for a writer.

In the event you hire a researcher to assist you in preparing an article or book, it's a good idea to have them sign a *Nondisclosure Agreement* before they start working for you. Such an agreement should read:

> *I, (the researcher), hereby acknowledge that I voluntarily accept disclosure by (the writer) regarding the story and/or book tentatively entitled (the title). This disclosure is made to me in confidence and with the understanding that it is not to be disclosed to others and it is not to be used by me for purposes beyond the limits of this confidence without the express, written permission of (the writer). I agree that all the ideas, storylines, characterizations, or other elements of the story that are related to me are the proprietary property of (the writer).*

There are two reasons for such an agreement, and one of them involves your legal protection. First, you want to discourage researchers from competing with you in the magazine or book business with what they've learned about your project. Secondly and importantly, you *might* be protecting yourself against a slander or libel suit for anything said or written by your researcher without your approval. This latter point is murky legal ground, though. I've had lawyers advise me that I'm ultimately responsible for any and all mistakes made by a researcher I've employed as long as I include those mistakes in my work. Just as a publisher is responsible for any mistakes made by a writer, I'm responsible for anything I cause to be published, even if I inadvertently violate someone's copyright by using plagiarized words and adaptations passed along by my researcher as his or her work. (This is one reason I don't include a researcher's writings in my own work. The best use of researchers is to break ground at the library or courthouse for you; but when they hit gold, mine it yourself.) For these reasons, I don't often hire researchers. In the end, I can do the work better, and if it takes me longer to do the job, then at least I know that any miscues I will have to answer for will be mine alone.

By the way, I adopted the practice some years back of sending the publication (or, for a book, my agent) an invoice once my story has been accepted. I bill publishers for several reasons, the best one being that a writer gets paid faster at some publications when the editor has an invoice to pass along to the accounts-payable person. Also, there is added protection when the invoice states exactly what rights the magazine is buying—usually "First North American Serial." And invoices are a good way to keep a record of income for tax purposes. Here's a sample invoice:

Editor's name   *Date*

Publication

Address

Invoice # (number)

Article fee for (title of article) ....$ *(amount)*

Rights sold (1st, 2nd, serial, etc.) ....$ *(amount)*

Expenses...................................$ *(amount)*

Expense receipts attached:
(Itemization of expenses)

Total Due This Invoice.......................$ *(amount)*

Writer's name and address

Writer's Social Security or Employer's ID number

When photographs are involved, it is necessary to have a signed model release before using the picture for anything other than ordinary news coverage. The written consent of a minor (a person under eighteen years of age, in most states) is not valid: the signature of the parent or guardian is required. The best time for a model release to be signed is at the time the picture is taken. In the release, some consideration should be given—a token fee or the gift of a finished photo works fine. Here's an example:

For value received (name the consideration), the receipt and adequacy of which are hereby acknowledged, I hereby give (name of magazine, publisher, or photographer) the absolute right and permission to copyright and/or publish, and/or resell photographic portraits of me or pictures of me, or in which I may be included in whole or in part, for art, advertising, trade, or any other lawful purpose whatsoever.

I hereby waive any right that I may have to inspect and/or approve the finished product or the advertising copy that may be used in connection therewith, or the use to which it may be applied.

I hereby release, discharge, and agree to save (name of magazine, publisher or photographer) harmless from any liability by virtue of any blurring, distortion, alteration, optical illusion, or use in composite form, whether intentional or otherwise, that may occur or be produced in the making of said pictures, or in any processing tending toward the completion of the finished product.

Some publications have gotten into legal trouble by using photos of unidentified people to illustrate a story, such as showing a generic shot of patrons in a bar for a story about alcoholics. One major magazine put on its cover a picture of a black man dressed in a business suit who was carrying a briefcase to illustrate a story on unemployment among blacks. The man, a successful stockbroker, sued and won a judgment. *He* was not unemployed (he didn't even know his picture was being taken), and therefore the picture put him in a *false light.*

Many writers have a serious misconception about the use of photographs. They incorrectly think that if they have the permission of the person in the photo, in the form of an adequate model release, they are home free. But actually, that is only half the battle. What also must be acquired before a photo is published is the permission of the picture's *copyright owner.* Here's the unfortunate scenario that so often happens: A writer is doing a profile of an athlete. During an interview, the athlete's mother brings out a picture album that contains a fetching picture of the athlete as a young tyke. "Can I use this photo?" the writer asks. "Of course," says the mother, handing it over. Later, when the writer's publisher asks if he has secured permission to use the photo, he remembers the mother's OK and says yes. After the photo is published, the writer and publisher are sued by the person who took the picture. In most cases, the copyright owner is the photographer who took the picture, but it can also be an agency or collection to whom the photographer sold or transferred his copyright.

Locating the copyright holder of a photo can be tricky, but with a little shrewd detective work, it usually can be done. On many commercial photos, the photographer's name and business address will be printed on the reverse. Or the photo's subject may be able to supply you with the photographer's name and city, and a phone book can do the rest. If the photo was published, the publisher will probably be able to put you in touch with the copyright holder. When you know who owns the rights, you can begin the process of getting permission to reproduce the photo the same way as you would for written material explained earlier in this chapter. (See pp. 66-67 for details.)

One way that securing photo permissions can be made less complicated is through the services of a picture agency, also known as a stock photo house. Such agencies have hundreds of thousands of photos on file, and by paying the copyright owner out of their fee, they can assign the right to publish a picture. Also, agencies keep on file—or make sure their photographers do—model releases for pictures that are going to be used commercially. Therefore, though you might pay more than if you hunted the photographer down yourself, the agency has solved both your problems.

If you are unsure about the wording of a permission or release, ask for help. Various writers' groups have sample releases. You might also want to consult with a publishing attorney. Surely, an ill-conceived permission or release is worse than none at all.

9

FACT-CHECKERS AND LAWYERS

It wasn't that long ago that both magazines and book publishers would routinely put into print a manuscript once the editors were satisfied with its style and content. That's the way Hemingway and Fitzgerald and so many other writers over the years were treated. But that age of innocence in publishing has ended.

Magazines, even smaller ones, have research departments charged with checking a nonfiction writer's facts and verifying quotes. And book publishers routinely send manuscripts, fiction and nonfiction, to their lawyers for review. The reason for all this care and attention is that publishers can lose lawsuits if they are found to have published inaccuracies with a *reckless disregard of the truth,* which has been defined as little or no fact checking.

So, these days, the facts get checked. Learning how the fact-checking process works is important to a writer for two reasons. First, you will know what to expect when a researcher or editor calls and starts grilling you on the tiniest details in your manuscript. And second, no conscientious writer working today should count on other people to catch and correct his mistakes, so it's imperative that *you learn how to fact-check for yourself.*

The first time I went through the fact-checking process (in 1978), I felt as if I had been put through a food grinder. Angry because I didn't understand why I was being picked on, I was also hurt because nobody was taking my word for *anything*. Until that moment, I had been thoroughly enjoying my life as a writer. But the thought of having my facts checked for the rest of my life made me sorry that I had turned down Beneficial Finance's management trainee program some years back. All in all, it was an appropriate welcome to the world of fact checking.

Fact-checkers are a special breed of nitpickers who can be a writer's worst enemy or best friend, depending on how well you have researched your work and what backup material is made available to them. Research departments like printed backup material because it is easier to check. In the past, there was a tradition that if something had been printed before, it was probably safe to repeat. No more. In today's legal climate, publishers know it is dangerous to assume that because something made it into print it is accurate or went through a careful legal review.

While writing a regular column for *New West* magazine some years ago, I did numerous short takes about Synanon, an organization that started as a California-based drug rehabilitation program but later became a nasty cult whose members committed various improprieties, such as placing a rattlesnake inside the mailbox of an outspoken critic. Synanon, which had its own legal department composed of members who were bona fide attorneys, spread the word that it would sue any news media outlet that wrote *anything* critical of the group. *Time* magazine and NBC, among others, found out that Synanon's threat was a serious one. Once, just hours away from our deadline, the *New West* lawyer lamented to me: "Do you really have to write this about Synanon?" Our lawyer, protecting our corporate interests, would probably have preferred for us to honor Synanon's threat rather than subject the magazine to a possible legal onslaught. When I pointed out that much of the information he was concerned about had been previously published by a small northern California newspaper, the lawyer was clearly relieved, and my column ran intact.

Later, that newspaper, the Point Reyes *Light,* would win a Pulitzer Prize for its gutsy reporting on Synanon. And later, profiling the *Light's* editor for another magazine, I heard about how the newspaper received its own apparently sound legal advice: "Every Thursday night, I'd meet this college buddy of mine, who was a lawyer, at the pizza parlor down the road. I'd show him what we were going to run in this week's edition, and he'd read it and say, 'Great, go for it.' I'd spring for the pizza." I have often wondered what the magazine lawyer would have said about that kind of casual legal review. Interestingly, the *Light* was never sued, even though it made Synanon the target of more than a year of tough, investigative reporting. Why? "Probably because we were such a small fry," said one of the paper's award-winning writers. (*New West* was never sued by Synanon, either, but we were threatened with legal action several times by its team of lawyers.)

There is another point, more subtle, about the availability or unavailability of previously-published backup material. Your editor has probably given you the assignment because it is a new story or you have a fresh angle. Those preferences often conflict because, on many assigned subjects, there just isn't going to be a lot of printed backup material. So, while the editor is guiding you in one direction, the researchers are often pulling in another. "You mean you have *no* clips," more than one exasperated researcher has asked me. "That's right," I reply proudly. "No one's done the story before."

Here is a form letter that the research department of a major magazine sends to writers on assignment:

> *To verify the facts you present, we need your assistance. Please save all materials used as reference and background, including newspaper clippings, tape transcripts, books, legal documents, menus (for restaurant reviews), movie programs, and interview notes. If your notes or transcripts are lengthy, please mark the appropriate passages. As a general rule, if you used it for reference information, we need it as well. Also, list the names and phone numbers of the principal sources you have contacted. This does not mean we automatically call each of your sources. Obviously, there are times when journalistic discretion prohibits this. We will, of course, work closely with you in these areas.*

It's been my experience, however, that fact-checkers *do* regularly call your sources unless you can come up with a powerful reason that they shouldn't. A *Reader's Digest* researcher once spent *four hours* on the telephone with a key source in one of my stories.

Interestingly, I had interviewed him for only *two hours*. The thought of a researcher reading back a quote to a source prior to publication is enough to send shivers down the back of the most cautious writer. Sources often do not understand why their two-hour interview with you was boiled down to a single paragraph or so. And, of course, usually that paragraph represents the strongest statement made by the source after hours of gentle prodding by the writer. Understandably, more than one researcher has been met with, "That's not what I meant" or "Let me restate that."

When a source or subject refuses to confirm a quote, one of two things has happened: either the writer got the quote wrong or the subject has forgotten or purposely recanted. If a quick check of the writer's notes verifies the written version—and, obviously, if the writer concurs with his own notes *and* if the publication trusts the writer—then most publications will feel safe to go with the disputed quote. Sometimes, a source may simply be sorry for telling the writer something—which is *not* grounds to delete or change a quote. In such a case, it is possible at times for the writer to reach a compromise with the source and come up with a new quote. But if the original quote is a great one, don't give it up just because your source got cold feet. On the other hand, know that if you are sued, this source is not going to be a good witness for you.

In addition to quotes, the fact-checkers verify such things as nouns and adjectives. (They usually let the writer slide on verbs.) Here's a recent discussion I had with a fact-checker at a major publication:

Fact-checker: You say the man is carrying a leather briefcase. How do you know that?

Me: Several people who had meetings with the man told me about his carrying the briefcase.

Fact-checker: OK, but was it leather?

Me: Well, they said it was an expensive brown briefcase. Is imitation leather expensive?

Fact-checker: That's not the point. *Was* it leather or *wasn't* it leather?

Me: Listen, if it will make you feel any better, you can delete leather. I don't think it will hurt the story any.

Fact-checker: Yes, that's what we'll have to do. *Leather* has to go.

What does it matter whether the briefcase was leather? Certainly no huge libel case will be won or lost on this point. But the research department's position on accuracy is that if you get the small things wrong in the article—like calling the Empire State Building 99 stories tall when everyone (?) knows it's actually 102 stories—how can you be believed on the major points of the story? Publication lawyers insist that such small mistakes *do* influence a judge and jury.

When your manuscript gets to the research department, a fact-checker will first want to go over your story with you. This can be done either in person or over the phone (just make sure the magazine is paying for the call). The fact-checker will want to know the source for virtually every fact. Sometimes, I prepare an annotated manuscript just for the researcher, with marginal notes that identify all my sources. For instance, adjacent to one paragraph I might say: "From Dr. Joe Smith. Phone 555-1234." This preliminary work prepares the researcher for the long haul ahead, and it makes the whole fact-checking procedure less time-consuming for the writer.

Some sources will be irritated by calls from researchers. I always try to make the event sound positive beforehand. "You will have a chance to verify everything and make sure I didn't make a mistake," I explain to my sources. Most of them appreciate having that chance. In fact, when someone asks to see my article before it's published (which, as I've already said, I never allow), I tell them that a researcher will be calling them to go over all the pertinent details. That usually satisfies the request for a review.

Fact-checkers work closely with the publication's attorneys. What the attorneys purportedly want in terms of backup will be relayed to you by a researcher. If you are confused by what the lawyers seem to be concerned about, ask to speak to them directly. In most cases, that will be no problem. It should be pointed out that at some publications, researchers tend to be junior editors. Sometimes a lack of experience on their part is offset only by a healthy dose of enthusiasm. So, don't cower and be afraid to speak your piece and defend your story. If you don't, who will?

Researchers should not make changes in your copy but will discuss problem areas and *recommend* changes to you and your editor. For instance, if *incompetent* seems too strong a word based on the information that was verifiable, the researcher might say to you, "How about using 'inefficient' instead?" Some writers fear that researchers are out to emasculate a story by lessening its impact. But a good researcher actually makes a story stronger by making it more defensible. And I've had more than one researcher turn the above example around by saying, "How about using 'incompetent' instead of 'inefficient'? We've got the backup for it."

A point to make here is that researchers are not writers. They are more the librarians of the business. They should not be making stylistic changes in your copy. The editors hired you, not the researcher, to do the writing. And presumably for a good reason. On the other hand, writers often need to have a check and balance. Some of us can get carried away with literary liberties and write exaggerations or even untruths without meaning to do so.

In cases of disputes between you and the fact-checkers, talk to your editor, who will not hesitate to step in and discuss the matter directly with the lawyers. Remember, the editor is just as worried as you are about editorial content and not disturbing the even flow of a piece. Sometimes an editorial judgment will override the recommendation of the research department. In fact, I've had editors who listened to both the researcher and the attorney and then did the exact opposite. After all, editors, not attorneys, are still putting out magazines and books. (I say this gratefully.)

It has been my experience that there are two types of attorneys who represent publications. The first is from what I call The Blank Page School. Like the lawyer who didn't want to take on Synanon, they would rather see nothing in print that will cause legal problems. As I see it, from their standpoint, the ultimate protection would be to run just that: *nothing.* No one ever sued over blank pages. But then, blank pages don't sell magazines or books, and that's the classic conflict that often develops between the editorial and legal camps. The other type of lawyers is the guys who will think of constructive ways and methods to tighten and strengthen the story. They understand that they're representing a business that has as its ultimate product *printed pages,* and they'll do everything they can to help figure out a safe and legal way for writers to say what they want to say.

Lawyers caution writers to separate their instincts, subjective feelings, and all those other intangibles from "hard evidence" when interviewing subjects and then, later, when sitting down to write. Any evidence that shows a writer intended to do harm to someone's reputation or image based on false information would be highly damaging in a lawsuit, whether the defendant is a public figure or a private citizen.

Articles and books are regularly killed because they fail the sort of verification and double-checking that is necessary today. (When I was an editor at *New West,* a cover article was killed at the last minute because it failed to get through the research department. Everyone scurried around to find another suitable cover story, because blank covers don't sell magazines either). Some magazines withhold payment until a story has made it through research; book publishers sometimes withhold the final advance payment until the legal questions have been resolved. These are some powerful incentives to work cooperatively and successfully with the fact-checkers and lawyers.

A consolation in dealing successfully with the researchers and lawyers is knowing that when they get through with your manuscript, it will be strong and verifiable and will stand up to legal challenges. And in case of a lawsuit, the researchers are witnesses for the defense, telling the judge and jury about all their efforts to verify the facts as you wrote them. In such situations, it's nice having company.

10

THE LAWSUIT

Despite doing everything right, you're sued.

Don't panic. Being sued happens to the best of us. If you've done your work well, you can properly defend yourself. If you haven't done your work well, then you have no one to blame but yourself.

As soon as you are served legal papers, contact the magazine or book publisher. Usually, they will have been named in the suit, too. Remember, you are all in this together. They need you to help them prove the integrity of your writing as much as you need them to pay the legal bills.

Some lawsuits are clearly frivolous and are eventually dropped by the plaintiff or dismissed by a judge before trial. But others go on and on. One of my more irksome lawsuits, an alleged copyright infringement case, resulted from an article I wrote about infamous plane hijacker D. B. Cooper, which was published in a men's magazine. After we were served, I asked the magazine for assurance that it would foot the legal bill. (Just a year or so earlier, another men's magazine had refused to defend two freelance writers in a lawsuit. The writers retained their own counsel, and prior to trial, made their own deal with the plaintiff that called for the writers to issue a letter of apology for some errors in their story in exchange for being dropped from the suit. One of the writers even showed up as a plaintiff's witness—and the magazine ended up losing the suit.) The magazine's house counsel gave me a letter of indemnification for legal fees and damages. The publisher retained one loophole: they would not defend me if at any time it came to their attention that I had been untruthful to them, such as in warranting the piece as my original work. In other words, if I *had* violated someone's copyright, I would be thrown overboard. That was fine with me because I knew I had done everything on the up and up.

The person suing had also investigated the well-known Cooper skyjacking case and had tried unsuccessfully to sell his own article and book on the subject. I quoted other people who were involved in his inquiry and named him in my story, too. I had interviewed him over the phone for more than an hour. The plaintiff claimed that I had infringed on his work, an unpublished manuscript that I had never seen until it was presented to the court. Interestingly, this article of mine had run in a Hearst magazine (with my copyright affixed to it) months earlier and was basically reprinted in the men's magazine. Although the plaintiff reportedly saw the newspaper version, he didn't sue until it ran in the men's magazine. Why? Because certain publications are considered "target defendants." Lawyers see them as having a bad reputation—which might make them vulnerable in front of a jury—as well as possessing lots of money to pay off nagging complaints.

We won the case when the judge ruled that the other side could prove none of its allegations. After nearly two years of maneuvers (including a full day I spent giving a deposition to the opposing attorney), our defense cost more than $10,000, and the bill was paid by the magazine.

In the rare case that a magazine publisher won't pay your legal bill, there are some other ways to gain free counsel. Finding an attorney who will handle the case *pro bono* (free) is not as hard as it might sound. What would be an attorney's motive for rendering free representation to a writer? Good publicity is one; social conscience is another. Twice, I've been represented by the American Civil Liberties Union because the cases involved the First Amendment issue of freedom of the press. Some attorneys have their own unique reasons for assisting a besieged writer. For a couple of years, I worked with a young attorney who wanted to learn more about copyright and publishing law (including reviewing contracts), and he didn't charge me for much of his time while learning his new specialty. It worked out well for both of us.

One cardinal rule: Never speak to a lawyer for the other side unless your lawyer is present. If the other side's lawyer calls you before you have representation, keep quiet and talk to (or find) your own lawyer. If the plaintiff's lawyer calls you *after* you have representation, report this serious breach of ethics to your attorney. These phone calls are fishing expeditions, in which the other side is trying to come up with information that could be used against you. Once again, I learned this lesson the hard way. I spent more than an hour talking to an attorney about his client's claim, and the result was the D. B. Cooper copyright infringement suit against me. Much of the information I had given this attorney ended up in the suit, though it was somewhat distorted to fit his client's side of the story. None of us has any business helping the other side engineer a lawsuit.

There is only one complete and unconditional defense a non-fiction writer has in a civil libel suit: that the facts stated are *provably* true. For instance, quoting someone accurately is not enough. If you are going to use a potentially libelous quote—like "That guy is a crook"—then it had better be true and you must be able to prove that it's true.

Another defense of libel is *privilege,* either qualified or absolute. You can claim *qualified privilege* (which is exceedingly limited and rare) if the social good of the community is served by publishing the information and if this overrides the damage done to an individual's reputation. *Absolute privilege* is your right to accurately quote an individual who is testifying at judicial and legislative hearings. However, be aware that privileges can be lost if there are errors in your writing. Once again, there is no substitute for accuracy.

The final defense a writer has in a libel action is claiming *fair comment and criticism.* We do have the right to comment on and criticize matters of public concern, such as in the writing of movie and restaurant reviews, even if in so doing we hurt someone's business or reputation.

Two decades ago, the U.S. Supreme Court made a series of rulings that were profoundly important in the area of libel. The result was that public figures cannot recover damages in a libel suit unless *actual malice* on the part of the writer can be proven. To establish malice, a plaintiff is required to prove that at the time of publication, those responsible for the story knew it was false or published it with reckless disregard of whether it was true or false. That means even if a writer makes a mistake, he can be spared losing a damage suit against a public figure. (You can see why so few public figures win libel suits.) Although the legal definition of what constitutes a public figure has been changed in recent years by U.S. Supreme Court decisions, the standard that exists now is that someone must "voluntarily" thrust himself into the news or before the public eye before he can be considered a public figure. In one disturbing 1979 case, the Supreme Court ruled that a man who had pleaded guilty to criminal contempt during a widely publicized espionage investigation was *not* a public figure. The majority of the court rejected the theory that "any person who engages in criminal conduct automatically becomes a public figure."

In the event that you discover after publication that you've made a mistake, having printed a timely and complete correction is paramount. A prompt correction might make it less likely that a wronged person will sue. Or, if a suit is filed anyway, it could prevent the plaintiff from being awarded hefty punitive damages. Of course, the best time to catch a mistake is before publication. But none of us is infallible; it's only fair that mistakes be admitted and the record set straight. In the case of newspapers and magazines, the correction or retraction should be made in the earliest possible edition or issue. (Interestingly, newspapers are not held as stringently responsible for the facts as are magazines. Because they have shorter deadlines, they can make and get away with more mistakes than magazines, which the courts feel have plenty of time to check for accuracy. A good example of this was Carol Burnett's lawsuit against the *National Enquirer*. A key skirmish concerned whether the weekly tabloid was a newspaper or a magazine. When the judge ruled it a magazine, thereby requiring additional fact-checking responsibilities, Burnett was able to win the decision.)

Correcting mistakes in books is more difficult. If the mistake is serious enough, the publisher may be forced to recall the entire printing. Though mistakes are more costly for book publishers, none of them has the fact-checking staff that so many magazines employ, and I've never understood why not. Of course, book publishers do send manuscripts out for legal review when the topic warrants it. While a publishing lawyer will identify critical areas and recommend that an editor question the writer in those areas about backup and source reliability, these reviews certainly are not as detailed as a magazine's fact-checking efforts.

A citizen's *right to privacy* is also used as grounds for lawsuits filed against writers. The intent of the law is the idea that a person has the right to be left alone, to live a private life free from publicity. But when a person becomes involved in a news event, voluntarily or involuntarily, the right to privacy is forfeited. The prison inmate who sued me as a result of my *Esquire* article claimed that I had invaded his right to privacy. In dismissing his suit, the court obviously felt that the fellow had forfeited his right to privacy when he committed the $10 million bank theft.

Newsworthiness of a subject has often been used by nonfiction writers as a defense against right-to-privacy actions. Indeed, a person's right to privacy sometimes conflicts with the public's right to know. But publications have lost such cases over articles that have dredged up sordid details of a person's past that had little or no newsworthiness. Publishing something that implies a person's commercial endorsement of a product is also an invasion of privacy.

Fiction writers can be hit by privacy suits, too. But, again, the plaintiff must prove "reasonable identification" first, and then convince the court that the reading public might ascribe the fictional character's more unsavory behavior and motivations to the real person's.

While we're on the subject of lawsuits, a particularly distressing development in the book business must be reported. "Most of the increased litigation we are seeing," says an attorney for a national authors' group, "is publishers' suits against authors." The majority of these actions are attempts by publishers to recover advances paid to authors who fail to turn in acceptable manuscripts. Obviously, the writer who signs a contract, receives an advance, and neglects to write a book deserves to be sued. But it is not always that simple. Some authors have found that their original editor is no longer working for the publisher when they turn in their manuscripts (editors do move around a lot), and the new editor rejects their effort and labels it unsatisfactory. Particularly when an editor is fired, the replacement seldom wants to be associated with the deposed predecessor's projects. The new editor's thinking might be: If the old editor got *fired,* how good can his projects and writers be?

Clearly, in such cases, writers should be protected from having to repay the advances. A few literary agencies are now negotiating for "nonreturnable advance" clauses in their contracts, but that might be a difficult sale to make. Another, more practical, way to protect yourself is to get a "first proceeds" clause in any book contract. That means that if the publisher declines to publish your manuscript, you have to pay back the advance only if and when you resell the project to another publisher. In that situation, you would want the second publisher's advance to be at least as large as the first one's so you'd have the money to pay back the first advance.

The good news in the book business these days is that many writers are being covered by their publishers' libel insurance policies, as was discussed earlier. Maybe, in time, this trend will carry over into the magazine arena.

I think it appropriate, however, that any chapter on lawsuits should end on a negative note. As reported in the *National Law Journal,* the Libel Defense Resource Center, which monitors libel cases in all fifty states, has calculated that juries find in favor of plaintiffs in 83 percent of libel cases, while plaintiffs in both medical malpractice and product liability cases win only half as often. Of course, this figure does not account for lawsuits that are dropped or dismissed before going to trial. But it is an ominous warning for writers everywhere, and it causes me to repeat this premise with emphasis: *Your best legal protection is to not be sued in the first place.*

11

INVESTIGATIVE REPORTING

Investigative reporting is a term that has been loosely thrown about in recent years. "It means to get someone," a journalism student replied when I once asked my class for a definition. Though that sometimes might result from a good bit of investigative reporting, a more accurate definition is *finding concealed information*.

Surprisingly, much "concealed" information can be found in public records and documents. "If they are public, how can they be concealed?" you might ask. Well, say a city councilman voted to allow a change of zoning on a parcel of property in order for a commercial shopping center to be constructed. That vote is certainly a matter of public record. Next, let's say the would-be shopping center owner is a corporation. A list of principal officers and other business information about the firm is available to the public. An investigative reporter on the trail of something might next look up the list of contributors to the councilman's last campaign. That, too, is public record. If the reporter finds that a corporate officer is listed as having given or loaned a big hunk of money to the councilman, he has the makings for a pretty decent investigative article for a local newspaper. And all of it came from public records. What makes it *concealed* is that no one put two and two together before to show that a sweetheart relationship existed between the councilman and certain members of the corporation.

Searching public records is tedious and time-consuming, but if something is wrong in city hall, some clue to it almost certainly will appear in public records if only you have the know-how, time, and imagination to find it. For investigative reporters, one nice thing about public records is that they usually can be checked anonymously. In other words, no one needs to know what you're looking for or whom you're investigating. The smaller the town, of course, the harder it might be to work unnoticed. But if a nosy clerk seems too interested in what you're doing (I sometimes worry that the target of an investigation might find out what I'm doing too early and try to dry up potential sources of information), then add a bunch of irrelevant names and property addresses to your list. The clerk will have fits trying to figure out a pattern to your work and will probably eventually give up.

Investigative reporting has been called a "precarious profession," and for good reason. There are certainly easier ways to make a living as a writer. For unless you are meticulous in developing and researching your story, and careful in writing it, you are likely to become a legal target. The subjects of your investigative efforts are seldom ordinary citizens; more likely, they are the rich and powerful and influential. They will hire lawyers and pounce on your every mistake and misjudgment, no matter how minor. You will find yourself in the unenviable position of having to defend virtually every word you write.

In a real sense, every writer will occasionally need to be an investigative reporter. That's why it's advisable for all practicing writers to know the various techniques used by journalism's top investigative reporters. Sources do not line up outside your front door waiting to be interviewed. Until they do, you will have to find them on your own. The information you need for a story or book is not going to be found in the Yellow Pages. Until the phone company devises a listing for "Literary Research—Retail," you'll have to know how to unearth what you need. And until the law schools of this country stop begetting lawyers like so many Kansas locusts, we should all know how to defend our every word.

When we choose to write about controversial subjects, we

start taking chances almost immediately. Writing a Tahiti travel piece or fashioning a profile of an Oscar-winning actor will usually (but not always) cause you less legal trouble than if you elect to use your writing as a force against abuses of power by your local councilman or senator.

One major difference between investigative reporting and other writing is that in the latter, you almost always know the angle that your piece is going to take before you get started. With investigative reporting, you almost never know what shape your story is going to take—or even if you are going to have a story—until you've expended quite a bit of time and effort. This is one reason investigative work is best done by a salaried staff writer or a freelancer who is guaranteed some payment. Ending up with no story at all, which happens occasionally, could be financially devastating to someone trying to make a living by writing.

In a typical investigative piece, the writer first has an inkling— but no solid proof—that something is not right. Even before you can figure out exactly what is not right, you need to identify all the players. In doing so, your research would usually include the following:

- *Checking domestic court files for marriages and divorces. Remember: Divorce proceedings will often spell out a person's financial picture. Also, ex-spouses can be highly motivated to spill the beans.*

- *Checking civil court cases for lawsuits filed by or against the people on your list. Again: Someone who has been at odds with a person in court might be willing and able to supply good inside information.*

- *Looking for drastic changes in economic status—sudden heavy real estate investments, heavy mortgages, a rash of bad-debt claims. A civil servant who spends more money than he makes might be ripe for a bribe.*

- *Looking for inconsistencies in behavior. A pro-environmentalist county supervisor suddenly approves a beachfront high-rise. Why? Is she on the take from the developer? Question motives, ask questions, but remember my earlier caution against committing slander.*

You face an added challenge in investigative work when you are regularly confronted by a source who is unwilling to talk, especially if he is involved in any of the alleged shenanigans. One way to handle such a situation is to say that unless he talks to you, you'll be forced to use the information supplied by others. The situation you like to set up is one in which everyone is bending over backwards to point a finger at someone else. Eventually, of course, you'll have to sort through the accusations and get to the truth of the matter. But the important thing at this stage is that you have a flow of information coming your way. Without information, you'll be left with only your suspicions, which every good investigative reporter starts with, but which, for ethical as well as legal reasons, have no business ending up in print.

By the way, I learned long ago that the most productive source for an investigative reporter is a middle-level bureaucrat or employee. Someone who is at the top, in management, for instance, is usually trying to protect his position and paycheck. And the lower-level people often aren't in a spot to get the goods on anyone higher up. The middle-ranked guys almost inevitably feel they can do the job better than their bosses, and they are close enough to the top to have an awareness of what's going on.

Investigative reporting is hard work. In carrying out a successful investigation of the local police department, a team of reporters for the *Indianapolis Star* managed to:

- *Develop as sources twenty-eight police officers, most of them beat cops who provided firsthand information, leads, and documents.*
- *Interview dozens of drug dealers and users, prostitutes, gamblers, and persons from all walks of life who had information on corruption in the department.*
- *Set up several observation posts, the most fruitful of which was a hotel room overlooking a pawnshop that was operated by a convicted fence. In one week alone, they photographed more than a dozen officers, including a deputy chief, leaving with gifts and cut-rate purchases.*

The series of stories that resulted won a host of local, state, regional, and national awards. Dozens of officers, from the chief of police on down, were fired, demoted, transferred, or encouraged to retire. Police department corruption was reduced, at least for the time being.

In such stories, *off-the-record* sources and *insiders* are important. Off-the-record information gets you on the right track and can lead to on-the-record sources. Insiders are also known as *whistle blowers*. They are tired of what they see going on and want reform, as did the honest officers of the Indianapolis police force.

Using records and documentation that can be brought into court in the event you are sued is a key to any investigative article. Rely on documents such as the following:

● *Subpoenas.* These are a fertile source of documented information about crime. These come from grand juries and are often made part of the public record.

● *Affidavits.* Filed in support of search warrants, arrests, or even when seeking permission to electronically eavesdrop, these usually become matters of public record in federal and state courts; they can provide good leads for articles.

● *Police arrest reports.* Don't forget the obvious. Unless sealed by a court order (which is rare), these reports are public record. They usually include the suspect's name and address, date of birth, sex, race, occupation, name of complainant (victim), time and place of arrest, name of arresting officer, type of crime, facts relating to the arrest, and witnesses.

Remember this about grand juries: What is said inside grand jury rooms is secret, but a witness who testified can walk out into the hallway afterward and repeat everything he said to his mother or a reporter without breaking the law. This is a good way to back-door a grand jury investigation. You just need to know the names of the witnesses who have been called, and then get in touch with them after their appearances.

Some years back, an informant approached two *Los Angeles Times* reporters and revealed that an investigation was under way into the dealings of a Burbank accountant who allegedly had bilked investors out of $10 million in a scheme involving phony imports from Hong Kong. The reporters tried to get details from authorities, but everyone was keeping quiet. (The reporters later found out why: some police officials were victims of the scam and had convinced other people to invest their money.) No one at the police department or the district attorney's office would talk. The reporters went to the

Burbank municipal court and looked through all the recent search warrants. They found the warrant for the accountant's records—there were other documents attached to it, including a complete list of victims with addresses and phone numbers. The reporters went out that afternoon and interviewed some victims, and an exclusive story ran in the following morning's newspaper.

Public officials are a popular target of investigative reporters. And well they should be, for when persons enter the political arena, they make themselves subject to intense scrutiny. They are asking us to elect them so that they can run our government. The public deserves to know whether they have any *conflicts of interest*—whether their official positions further their personal and financial interests. A public official's financial, professional, and in some areas, even personal life must be an open book. Here are some ways to open the book:

• *Financial reports.* People usually don't give money to a politician just for the fun of writing a check. They might just support a politician's stand on the important issues of our time, which is fine. But when they connect a contribution to delivering a vote or a favor, that is wrong. Four types of financial reports are available (in person and to the public) from the following offices:

1. The Federal Election Commission (FEC), Office of Public Records, 1325 K Street NW, Washington D.C. 20463. All presidential, senatorial, and congressional candidates' reports since 1972 are on file here. You'll also find reports from 2,000 PACs (Political Action Committee) that contribute to federal candidates. The FEC also has accumulated the best publicly available reports for the years before 1972 (less detailed, though, because of a lack of strong financial reporting laws and may also have reports from local political groups that are exempt from state reporting requirements.

2. The Secretary of the U.S. Senate, Office of Public Records, 119 D Street NW, Washington D.C. 20510. Senate candidates file the originals of their reports here. (The FEC will have copies, though.)

3. The Clerk of the U.S. House of Representatives, Office of Records and Registrations, Room 1036, Longworth House Office Building, Washington D.C. 20515. House candidates file the originals of their reports here. (The FEC will have copies.)

4. The Office of the Secretary of State or its counterpart in each state. Reports for state and local candidates are on file here, as well as some federal PACs based in an individual state. Local candidates deserve scrutiny, too.

● *Voting records.* The Democratic Congressional Campaign Committee keeps a compilation of voting records for incumbents of both parties. It is one thing for a politician from a cotton-growing state to vote for subsidies for cotton growers; that's expected. It is quite another to file an immigration bill in order to help a Columbian drug smuggler who wants to come to the United States. You should question an action like that and try to find out the extent of the connection between the two or how much money the smuggler paid the politician for the favor. Remember, don't stop your scrutiny after the election. Once a politician is in office is when favors start getting paid back. To check voting records, go to the library and look in *Politics in America, The Almanac of American Politics* or *Congressional Directory* (most valuable).

● *Personal life.* If you are looking for evidence that a politician has pocketed campaign money and spent it on personal things, look for records that show he's living beyond his means—boat and airplane registrations, fancy cars bought for cash (no lienholder on vehicle registration), lavish vacations, summer homes and other real estate (property records). Compare expenses to salary; if he spent more than he took in, you have some interesting questions to ask. And don't forget routine checks like divorce records. A former U.S. senator and a former state attorney general both got into campaign financial trouble when their estranged wives reported more financial information to the divorce court than the officials had reported to the Federal Election Commission.

Only after you have all the documentation you can find should you attempt to interview the target of your investigation. Prior to that, you might be bluffed or misled by evasive answers to your questions. But when you have the goods on someone, it is harder for him to squirm out from under you. In describing this timing, I have often used a wolf analogy. You pick off the little people on the periphery first. Then, gradually you circle in for the kill, just like the wolf. Your target will usually sense that you are coming. He may panic or threaten you, which is a good sign that you have something. He may not talk to you. But he may also be so psyched out that he'll confess at least some parts of the scheme. You might pretend to have more information than you actually do and cause him to reveal new details to you. If he's done something wrong, he will be sitting in fear that you know everything. The other reason for going to your target last: You might not get a second shot at him. Suppose you go to him too early and a subsequent interview with someone else arms you with more information and questions? Your target might not sit still for you again.

Everything we've covered so far assumes that you're going to be tackling your subject head-on, and that you'll be identifying yourself as you go along. In another method of investigative reporting, *undercover journalism,* a reporter goes undercover, using a false identity and misrepresenting himself, in order to get a story. Much criticism and controversy has been leveled at publications and writers who have used this technique. Only a slim majority of professional editors believe that if there is no other way to get a story, undercover journalism is acceptable.

There are some ground rules in this type of reporting. First, you should always try to get the story without resorting to trickery. And then, once a decision has been made for you to masquerade as something other than a journalist, your actions should be carefully monitored by other professionals who can later testify to your integrity. One concern: that you didn't entrap someone into doing something wrong that you will later report on. Another: that you don't break any laws yourself. In journalism, the end does not justify the means. We have to keep ourselves at a higher level than those we're accusing of dastardly deeds.

A classic example of undercover journalism was the "Mirage" series by the *Chicago Sun-Times.* The newspaper set out to prove that bribery was fundamental to Chicago's life and government. Obviously, the reporters couldn't very well get damaging information from people who were involved in giving or receiving bribes. Instead, they got their story in a unique way. They rented storefront business space and set up a new business, a corner bar, in the downtown neighborhood. Soon, all sorts of officials, from beat cops to building inspectors, began showing up and demanding bribes in turn for doing favors for the new bar owners. A video camera hidden behind a wall documented the payments of cash and liquor. The disguise was creative, audacious, and successful. After a month in business, the bar was closed and the newspaper began its long series, which was informative as well as fun to read. Though the series rocked city hall and set the stage for a "reform" mayor, the "Mirage" series did not win a Pulitzer Prize. (However, many newspapers around the country, including the paper's cross-town competitor, the *Chicago Tribune*, thought it should have.) During deliberations of the Pulitzer Prize Board, there was heated argument. The major objection to honoring the series was the fact that what was seen as deception was used to get the story. *Washington Post* editor Ben Bradlee was quoted at the time: "We would never allow reporters to misrepresent themselves in any way and I don't think we would be the hidden owners of anything." Another editor and member of the Pulitzer Board said: "The board pretty generally came down on the side of saying, yes, there can be times when the overwhelming needs of the public justify it. But on the opposite side of the coin, if there is any other way of discovery, this should be the last resort." The board voted ten to two against "Mirage," and the story was dropped from consideration.

Finally, undercover work is dangerous. If your true identity is discovered by a crooked cop or crooked anybody, you could be in trouble. For this reason, *never do undercover work on your own.* Have a publication behind you, and at least one person who knows where you are—or better yet, is observing you—at all times.

A safer way to get information for an investigative article is by utilizing the Freedom of Information Act (FOIA). The intent of this act—first passed into law in 1966 but substantially amended (and strengthened in our favor) in 1974—is to provide public access to information gathered and stored by the federal government. The three major provisions of the FOIA state that:

1. Every agency subject to the Act (including the FBI) must publish its address, phone number, and names of executives in the Federal Registry (to help people find out who has the records they need).

2. Agencies must make available final opinions and orders (from court cases), statements of policy, and administrative staff manuals and instructions with an index.

3. Agencies must make available upon request *reasonably described* records. This is the most important provision for writers. You must have a fairly specific idea of what it is you are seeking in order to meet this provision.

Once you have made your request to a specific agency, the agency has ten days to answer or notify you that your request has been denied, giving the reason for the denial. You can then appeal the agency's decision. Nine categories of information are excluded, such as personnel matters, records that affect national security, or interagency letters and memorandums. Obviously, you should allow for delays.

Following are some tips for requesting information under the FOIA:

- *Don't make an FOIA request unless you absolutely need to. Try to get the information another way if possible. It is obviously much quicker to get documents other ways. Also, a fair percentage of FOIA requests are denied. Remember, you are dealing with bureaucratic red tape.*
- *Make your request as precise as possible; the government can refuse requests that are overly broad.*
- *Use the telephone exclusively to determine what government office has the information that you seek.*
- *Before filing a FOIA request, check the agency's FOIA reading rooms (in Washington, D.C.) to find out whether someone has already made the same request. If so, you can read it there and save your time and expenses. The Department of Defense, for example, has a computer printout of about 1,200 previously fulfilled FOIA requests you can look at.*
- *For further information, send away for "How to Use the Federal FOIA Act," a twenty-four-page comprehensive pamphlet by The Reporters Committee for Freedom of the Press, Suite 300, 800 18th Street NW, Washington D.C. 20006.*

12

FINAL DOS AND DON'TS

A few years ago, I was being interviewed on a live radio program in Los Angeles about a cover article I had written for *California* magazine. The article was about a small group of corrupt police officers who had burglarized businesses while working the graveyard shift in Hollywood. The cover illustration was sufficiently sensational, showing a uniformed cop standing between two scruffy-looking hoods in a police lineup. (Obviously, all three were professional models and the picture was staged in a photo studio.)

As you would expect, a lot of fact checking and legal review went into this article because we were making some serious charges and naming names along the way. My concern as I went on the talk show was to remember to limit my remarks strictly to the information that appeared in the article. To help me do so, I kept a copy of the article in front of me, with certain points highlighted.

"Now, did these Hollywood police officers know what was going on?" I heard the radio announcer ask.

"Oh, yes," I answered confidently. "They knew what was going on because they were part of it."

The next day, when I listened to a tape recording of the interview, I realized that the announcer had actually asked: "Did the *other* Hollywood police officers know what was going on?"

Some three hundred officers were assigned to the Hollywood precinct. About ten of them were involved in the burglary ring. But in misunderstanding the question, I had implied that *all of them* had taken part in the illegalities. In other words, I had slandered approximately two hundred and ninety police officers.

In a panic, I telephoned the magazine's lawyer. "Should I call the radio station and ask them to run a correction?" I asked.

The lawyer wanted to know if the magazine or I had received any calls. The answer was no. "Let's wait and see," the lawyer said. "Maybe the listening audience heard the question the same way you did."

It turned out to be sound advice because we never received a single complaint, and possibly by publicly apologizing we would have just amplified the mistake. This unfortunate episode illustrates a problem for writers, one that is aggravated by the expectation publishers have these days that we'll help promote articles and sell books. Inevitably, a writer knows more about a story than what makes it into print. But much of that excess information is speculative and unverifiable—if it were strong and verifiable, it would probably be in the story. During a live interview it can be difficult to limit yourself to just the published information, especially for someone like me who is accustomed to expressing himself by the written— not spoken—word. But failure to do so could result in a slander suit, and what terrible irony that would be after laboring so hard to avoid a libel suit.

Two of the nicest words in the English language are *reportedly* and *allegedly*. Use them whenever it is appropriate. There are ways to state something as a fact ("He stole the money") and ways to hedge something ("He allegedly stole the money"). There's a big difference. If you saw somebody steal something and can prove it, or if that person has been *convicted* of theft, then you can say, "He stole the money." If someone has only been *accused* of stealing, then you must say, "He allegedly stole the money."

Publication lawyers are on the lookout for certain red-flag words that can get a writer in trouble. In a very helpful pamphlet, *Synopsis of the Law of Libel and the Right of Privacy*, available from World Almanac Publications, author Bruce W. Sanford offers a sampling of such words and phrases, including: *intimate, atheist, com-*

munist, fascist, crook, fraud, and *alcoholic.* But you must also watch out for the infamous *bag lady, acid freak, lush, AIDS* (or *cancer*), and *dishonest,* and all the ethnic/religious slurs Archie Bunker got away with but writers can't.

Basically, if you say anything that implies someone has a fatal or loathsome disease; has committed a crime or associates with criminals; or is a social undesirable, an ignorant yokel (urban or rural), minority scum, or a person it wouldn't be wise to buy a car from or lend five dollars to, you've given an open invitation to legal challenge.

But avoiding particular red-flag words in itself won't keep you out of trouble. The context you put something in is every bit as important as the actual words you use. "He took without permission" will land you in court every bit as fast as "He stole." So use your common sense. Think before you write, and weigh every word as the target for a potential lawsuit before what you write is published. If what you say is true, you may have to *prove* it; if it's untrue, or just not provable, you may find yourself eating not only your words, but a whopping court award.

When writing nonfiction, you are allowed no areas of fantasy. Once, I had to explain in court papers how I knew a subject of one of my magazine articles had actually squeezed lemon on a caviar omelet. The subject had sued me for libel and listed more than three hundred alleged examples of inaccuracies (going to the issue of "careless disregard of the truth"), including this one. But I had *not* fabricated the lemon squeezing; I had learned about it from someone who sat across from the subject at the breakfast in question. Silly, you say? My lawyer warned that we had to defend every one of those examples. If we had let forty or fifty of the silly ones slide by, the plaintiff might begin to build a case of faulty and inaccurate writing, which in the end might have translated to my first courtroom loss. (It didn't, because we were able to document and verify everything in the article.)

In these pages, I've related a lot of horror stories for writers. How many of you have been scared off and have already signed a homesteading deed to protect the equity in your home (I have), or decided that writing can be dangerous? This discourse was not meant to discourage, but rather to inform. Writing is a serious business, and the potential we all have for abusing our power is frightening.

In *Los Angeles* magazine, I label a man an infamous con artist and 300,000 readers now consider him a crook. In *TV Guide*, I accuse a movie studio of withholding an actor's money and 20 million readers now think of that studio in a negative light. I tell the story of a woman's being convicted as a large-scale child pornographer in *Reader's Digest* and 50 million readers consider her one of the most vile people to walk the face of the earth. I write a book about a bank officer who embezzled $21 million from his employer—I can go on and on. I have made these unqualified allegations, but only after *carefully researching the facts* and being sure I was on solid ground. In none of the above-mentioned cases was I sued. I consider that a matter of neither luck nor chance, but rather an exhibition of intelligent and factual reporting that resulted in careful and verifiable writing.

You see, in all those cases, I had bulletproofed my manuscripts.

Index

About the Author

Freelance writer Bruce B. Henderson contributes regularly to *Reader's Digest* and has had articles published in such magazines as *Playboy*, *Esquire*, *TV Guide*, *Family Weekly*, and *California*. He is also the coauthor of *Empire of Deceit* (Doubleday), a nonfiction book about a bank heist, and has written a novel and two additional nonfiction books. He has taught hundreds of writing students at three California universities, produced and written for television newsmagazine shows, and served as associate editor for *New West* magazine. In his more than sixteen years as a writer, he has been sued just three times—and has never lost a suit.

Other Books of Interest

General Writing Books

   Getting the Words Right: How to Revise, Edit and Rewrite, by Theodore A. Rees Cheney $13.95

   How to Get Started in Writing, by Peggy Teeters (paper) $8.95

   How to Write a Book Proposal, by Michael Larsen $9.95

   How to Write & Sell Your Personal Experiences, by Lois Duncan (paper) $9.95

   How to Write & Sell (Your Sense of) Humor, by Gene Perret (paper) $9.95

   How to Write While You Sleep, by Elizabeth Ross $12.95

   Law & the Writer, edited by Polking & Meranus (paper) $10.95

   Knowing Where to Look: The Ultimate Guide to Research, by Lois Horowitz $16.95

   Pinckert's Practical Grammar, by Robert C. Pinckert $12.95

   The 29 Most Common Writing Mistakes & How to Avoid Them, by Judy Delton $9.95

   Writer's Block & How to Use It, by Victoria Nelson $12.95

   Writer's Guide to Research, by Lois Horowitz $9.95

   Writer's Market, edited by Becky Williams $21.95

Magazine/News Writing

   Basic Magazine Writing, by Barbara Kevles $16.95

   How to Sell Every Magazine Article You Write, by Lisa Collier Cool $14.95

   Writing Nonfiction that Sells, by Samm Sinclair Baker $14.95

Fiction Writing

   Creating Short Fiction, by Damon Knight (paper) $8.95

   Fiction Writer's Market, edited by Jean Fredette $18.95

   Handbook of Short Story Writing, by Dickson and Smythe (paper) $8.95

   How to Write & Sell Your First Novel, by Oscar Collier with Frances Spatz Leighton $14.95

   Writing the Modern Mystery, by Barbara Norville $15.95

   Writing the Novel: From Plot to Print, by Lawrence Block (paper) $8.95

Special Interest Writing Books

   The Craft of Comedy Writing, by Sol Saks $14.95

   How to Make Money Writing About Fitness & Health, by Celia & Thomas Scully $16.95

   How to Write the Story of Your Life, by Frank P. Thomas $12.95

   Nonfiction for Children: How to Write It, How to Sell It, by Ellen E.M. Roberts $16.95

   The Poet's Handbook, by Judson Jerome (paper) $8.95

   Poet's Market, by Judson Jerome $16.95

   Travel Writer's Handbook, by Louise Zobel (paper) $9.95

   TV Scriptwriter's Handbook, by Alfred Brenner (paper) $9.95

   Writing for Children & Teenagers, by Lee Wyndham (paper) $9.95

The Writing Business

   Complete Guide to Self-Publishing, by Tom & Marilyn Ross $19.95

   How to Get Your Book Published, by Herbert W. Bell $15.95

   How to Understand and Negotiate a Book Contract or Magazine Agreement, by Richard Balkin $11.95

   Literary Agents: How to Get & Work with the Right One for You, by Michael Larsen $9.95

   Professional Etiquette for Writers, by William Brohaugh $9.95

To order directly from the publisher, include $2.00 postage and handling for 1 book and 50¢ for each additional book. Allow 30 days for delivery.

Writer's Digest Books, Dept. B, 9933 Alliance Rd., Cincinnati OH 45242
Prices subject to change without notice.